Catalytic Conversations

Catalytic Conversations

Organizational Communication and Innovation

Ann C. Baker

M.E.Sharpe
Armonk, New York
London, England

This book is dedicated to
Charlotte Anne

Library of Congress Cataloging-in-Publication Data

Baker, Ann C.
  Catalytic conversations : organizational communication and innovation / by
Ann C. Baker.
      p. cm.
  Includes bibliographical references and index.
  ISBN 978-0-7656-1280-9 (cloth : alk. paper) — 978-0-7656-1281-6 (pbk. : alk. paper)
  1. Communication in organizations. 2. Interorganizational relations. I. Title.

  HD30.3.B3635 2009
  658.4′5—dc22   2009027443

Printed in the United States of America

The paper used in this publication meets the minimum requirements of
American National Standard for Information Sciences
Permanence of Paper for Printed Library Materials,
ANSI Z 39.48-1984.

∞

IBT (c)   10   9   8   7   6   5   4   3   2   1
IBT (p)   10   9   8   7   6   5   4   3   2   1

Contents

Part I

1

Introduction

Could the health of an organization hinge on something as commonplace as talk? Taking conversations for granted is not unusual, but they are integral to work and play and are a hub of organizational life. Conversations are the channel through which people work with others, make decisions, and build relationships. Much as the air we breathe, we often do not pay much attention to the quality of our conversations until they deteriorate or we lose connections with others completely. As with the air, it is easy to forget the magnitude of good conversation until it is toxic or in short supply.

This book is for people working in, learning about, and researching organizations. It addresses how to enhance the quality and viability of groups and organizational life by paying attention to how people talk—and do not talk—to each other. Although some conversations support organizational enhancement, others inhibit it. I distinguish among many aspects of conversation and show how conversations and organizational well-being are inseparable from continuous change and learning. Similarly, I emphasize how conversations are at the heart of creating new knowledge and are therefore precursors to sustainable change and innovation.

The word *conversation* in this book refers to exchanges among people. These exchanges may be verbal, nonverbal, or written, and they may occur in person or in other contexts, such as conference calls and via the Internet. My focus is on conversation as a medium through which people increase or block their understanding of each other and create new knowledge together. I propose that conversation can fundamentally improve an organization by providing entrée into transformative change.

Catalytic Conversations

My use of the word *catalytic* is intentional. By definition, a catalyst inspires and provokes fundamental change with less energy than would be possible without it. A catalyst, therefore, is expansive. Catalytic conversations are at the core of a new worldview and thus are key ingredients to revitalizing people and organizations.

When catalysts bring about change in chemical reactions it is not always possible to understand exactly how they work because of the dynamic complexity of multiple influences that vary across contexts (*Encyclopedia Britannica Online* 2007). Similarly, in a catalytic conversation the exact source or point of change is not fully understandable. The process of using catalytic conversations can seem a little mysterious because of this ambiguity and lack of predictability. Therefore, rather than becoming bogged down in understanding the mechanics of catalytic conversations, I focus on how to encourage and use them and their role in conversational learning. Organizations, groups of people, and individuals can create contexts that invite and reinforce catalytic conversations. Gaining insight into what we can do to encourage catalytic conversations, listening that leads to substantive change, constructive controversy, and new knowledge creation is the purpose of this book.

In catalytic conversations, people explore differences—that is, of opinion, values, experience, expertise, points of view—and look at them from a variety of vantage points. Together they uncover new aspects of issues or situations they had not been aware of before and consider them in a new light by gaining more information and broader understanding. When minds open to novel insights and perspectives, people are often able to imagine alternatives they had not previously realized.

A catalyst in a conversation can take many forms. It can come into view as a burning curiosity, trusting relationship, provocative idea, unfamiliar words, timely story, previous experience, unconditional acceptance, new information, another's patience, or possible hope. Throughout this book, I will elaborate and suggest how these forms serve as catalysts.

When we hear a story that especially resonates with us in the moment, it grasps our attention and encourages us to pay close attention and ask questions. When we are in a trusting relationship, we are more likely to ask questions, take risks, and ask for help even if doing so might reveal vulnerability (Edmondson 1999). Often the catalyst—trust, respect, curiosity, acceptance, or patience—creates a conducive environment for people to stretch beyond their typical comfort level and thus sparks creative interactions and new insight.

Without the catalyst, people are more likely to avoid substantive conversation or to lapse into monologues or arguments when they encounter differences. Pulled in by the catalysts, people become intrigued enough to want to hear more and the door to increased understanding begins to open a bit. Rather than suppressing diverse experiences and opinions, catalytic conversations make use of them as a source of interest; a source of energy. One of the crucial challenges in catalytic conversations is to be engaged in a mode of inquiry, as opposed to reacting or blindly advocating a position. In catalytic conversations participants take the time to ask questions, listen to responses, share experiences and share stories to illustrate ideas, and access intuitive and tacit knowledge. By working through these conversations with others, participants cultivate relationships of respect and trust, which in turn provide the foundation and incentives for more catalytic conversations and wide-ranging conversational learning.

Because contemporary organizational life is never static and a catalyst stimulates even more change, conversations frequently take place in rapidly changing, even tumultuous, environments. Fast-paced interactions give people less time to absorb and make sense of what a speaker intended. Such environments and pace may make one wonder whether catalytic conversations are beyond reach. Many people think they do not have time for an in-depth conversation and are not sure how other people will react if they try to engage in one. Yet these people fail to realize that conversations are a key to working more effectively. Conversation is the primary medium of work, especially in a knowledge-intensive world. By facilitating collaboration and understanding, catalytic conversations make it easier to learn how to anticipate change by providing a foundation of knowledge in the midst of a world of ambiguity.

Suppose you and I are working for an organization on a project team that is under considerable pressure. If I know you have expertise that is different from my own and if I feel we can trust each other to work toward our mutual self-interest and the success of the project, I am much more likely to try to collaborate with you and less likely to be competitive. By getting off to a good start by trying to encounter our differences as potential catalysts to learning, we can more readily help each other be successful while also adding value to the organization.

Having a catalytic conversation does not mean that people necessarily agree with each other or give up their own concerns, self-interests, values, or worldviews. It does mean that such conversations can shed new light on situations and ideas. They facilitate better understanding about "where someone else is coming from." They can open a window into the complexity of those with whom we disagree so that we understand them better and recognize their motivation. The process enables people to discover common ground and build common goals more easily.

The capacity to have catalytic conversations is not a technique to decipher, master, or prescribe. It is less about specific actions than it is about intentionally engaging with others to both speak and really hear, to both influence and be influenced. These kinds of conversations do not occur often without deliberate effort, considerable discipline, and clarity of purpose—that is, being intentional. The conversations are not necessarily logical because they engage all aspects of an individual, drawing upon cognitive and interpersonal dimensions, upon the head and the heart. Thus, to stay engaged in ways that encourage others also to remain involved, participants need to develop the patience to ask questions and deeply listen to the responses as they try to build on one another's thoughts and ideas.

A common misunderstanding is to assume that catalytic conversations are a kind of active listening or to assume that active listening is adequate. Instead, I am proposing a profoundly different approach. In catalytic conversations, people need to listen while remaining open to influence by others so they can learn together. In other words, if I want you to understand me better, I have to mirror that intention through seeking to understand you. If I want to influence you, I must be open to being influenced by you. These asking, listening, and building behaviors are so central to the nature of catalytic conversations that I refer to them repeatedly and offer examples of them throughout the book.

When this overall process becomes a part of the norm and culture of a group or organization, the participants are engaged in conversational learning (Baker, Jensen, and Kolb 2002; Wyss-Flamm 2003). Conversational learning shifts the responsibility for the communication away from one or a few people to a prevailing norm of broad inclusiveness and shared responsibility. This book explores many facets of such communication and the contexts needed to support them. It calls for developing the *art* of conversation while appreciating its power and its fragility.

This book is also especially timely in a world facing economic, environmental, and international crises with a new president in the White

House. A living example is unfolding on the world stage offering rich manifestations of the challenges and opportunities embedded in having the strength to be open to listening, talking, and working with diverse others in new ways. After all, this approach has always been at the heart of diplomacy and professional integrity.

Conversations and Differences in Organizations

Several analysts have discussed the importance of conversations in organizations. Ford and Ford (1995) point out that organizational change occurs through conversation. William Isaacs says that what people most need is to "rediscover the art of talking together" and how to "think together in relationship" (Issacs 1999, xx and 19). According to Patricia Shaw (2003), "the activity of conversation itself is the key process through which forms of organizing are dynamically sustained and changed" (p. 10).

Alan Webber (1993), formerly a managing editor of the *Harvard Business Review* and a founding editor of the magazine *Fast Company,* takes the analysis a step further:

> the most important work in the new economy is creating conversations . . . But all depends on the *quality* of the conversations. . . . Conversations—not rank, title, or the trappings of power—determine who is literally and figuratively "in the loop" and who is not. (p. 28; emphasis added)

The pervasiveness of conversation is increasingly apparent through blogs, Twitter, and many other social networking mediums on the Internet as well as through expanding collaborative technologies. Conversations enable people to be "in the loop" at the individual, group, and organizational levels. This book emphasizes the importance of creating *quality* conversations.

This book builds on previous work in this area and adds critical new dimensions. Uppermost, it focuses specifically on differences among people and the importance of integrating, not diminishing, the integrity of diverse perspectives and interpretations. Each person's perspective is a part of the organizational milieu as the verbalized and silent perspectives collectively give shape to organizational environments. Upbeat, discouraging, methodical, and passive perspectives all have influence and contribute to the work milieu. Therefore, the parties involved in the conversation and its development are critical. This book challenges an all too common perception that differences between people are an organizational problem to overcome or avoid. Instead, I delve into how differences can be positive resources for organizations to prompt learning, adaptation, flexibility, innovation, and improved quality.

For instance, suppose that you and I attend an important meeting together in our organization. After it is over, if you describe what happened in the meeting and I describe the same meeting it is likely that the descriptions would be at least somewhat different as we each try to make sense of what occurred. Alternatively, we might leave the meeting with fundamentally differing perspectives. A critical distinction is whether our differences are about *facts* or are about *perspectives* and *opinions*.

If we were to engage in a catalytic conversation and talk about more concrete factual differences, we would be likely to uncover information that one of us has and the other does not or information that neither of us has. We might talk about things that do not make sense to us that could result from missing data.

On the other hand, our differing perspectives would emerge. By exploring these ambiguous differences in a spirit of inquiry, new insights and unanticipated possibilities would come to the surface. I might begin to accept your interpretation. Yet I would not have to agree with you to realize that your perspective is a vital part of the milieu within which we work. Figuring out which of our perspectives is "right" and which is "wrong" is probably not possible—and I suggest that it may not be desirable. Instead, new understanding and insight broadens each of our personal perspectives.

If a conversation is one of advocacy rather than inquiry, it is more likely to involve each person trying to convince, or silence, the other. From an organizational perspective, trying to get everyone to see the world the same way requires condensing diverse perspectives into a homogenized view. It drains organizations and people of vital talent, information, resources, and energy. Brown and Duguid (2000), Nonaka (1994), Rycroft and Kash (1999), and Wenger (1998) have shown that it diminishes innovation, learning, and knowledge creation and leaves organizations in a knowledge-intensive world at a dramatic disadvantage. Conversely, catalytic conversations help participants distinguish between necessary facts on one hand and the differing priorities, values, and opinions that well-intentioned people bring into the organization on the other.

Even when people strongly disagree, if they are intentional about how they talk with one another and stay engaged in ongoing conversations, they can learn more about how and why they see things differently even though they may rarely gain complete insight. Conversations that incorporate differences generate learning and broader understanding, which are fundamental to thriving organizations and can spawn innovation (Argyris 1997; Baker et al. 2002; Isaacs 1999; Rycroft and Kash 1999).

References

Argyris, C. 1997. *On organizational learning*. Malden, MA: Blackwell Publishers Inc.

Baker, A. C., P. J. Jensen, and D. A. Kolb. 2002. *Conversational learning: An experiential approach to knowledge creation*. Westport, CT: Quorum Books.

Brown, J. S., and P. Duguid. 2000. *The social life of organization*. Boston: Harvard Business School Press.

Edmondson, A. 1999. "Psychological safety and learning behavior." *Administrative Science Quarterly* 44: 350–383.

Encyclopedia Britannica Online. 2007. http://search.eb.com/article-49417 (accessed December 30, 2007).

Ford, J. D., and L. W. Ford. 1995. The role of conversations in producing intentional change in organizations. *Academy of Management Review* 20: 541–570.

Isaacs, W. 1999. *Dialogue and the art of thinking together*. New York: Currency.

Nonaka, I. 1994. A dynamic theory of organizational knowledge creation. *Organization Science* 5 (1): 14–37.

Rycroft, R. W., and D. E. Kash. 1999. *The complexity challenge: Technological innovation for the 21st century*. New York: Pinter.

Shaw, P. 2003. *Changing conversations in organizations: A complexity approach to change*. New York: Routledge.

Webber, A. M. 1993. What's so new about the new economy? *Harvard Business Review* (January-February): 24–42.

Wenger, E. 1998. *Communities of practice: Learning, meaning, and identity*. New York: Cambridge University Press.

Wyss-Flamm, E. D. 2003. Conversational learning in teams: A dynamic model for individual and group development. Paper presented at the annual meeting of the Academy of Management, Seattle, Washington.

2

Organizing and Innovating through Conversations

The term *organization* as used in this book refers to groups of people in relationships with each other who have common interests or shared purposes, rather than to fixed structures or organizational charts. Even though the term *organization* most commonly engenders images such as hierarchies and structures, my interest is in the organiz*ing*—that is, the ongoing interactions between and among people doing the work. Through their work and conversations, people in organizations create structures, hierarchies, procedures, rules, customs, and norms, all of which encourage some behaviors and discourage others.

Perceptions of Organizations

People from Western nations, and especially in North America, are generally predisposed to take a "rational" approach to addressing the challenges of the workplace.[1] For example, when an organization in the United States calls on consultants to help when the organization is no longer maintaining its competitiveness, the consultants typically use quantitative methodologies, such as statistical analyses, closed-answer questionnaires, and other rational methods, to diagnose the problems.

These rational approaches do not readily access information about complex human interactions and the underlying reasons for behaviors. A more comprehensive approach to addressing the issues would include ethnographic observation, interviews, and other qualitative, less rational approaches, because not all human behavior is rational. The advantage of using processes that are more relational and contextual is that data can be gathered that is more relevant to the nuanced aspects of organizational challenges and the ongoing interactions between the people at the heart of organizational work.

Another limitation of an exclusively rational approach is a tendency of recommendations for change to focus on narrow aspects of the issues, which are often symptomatic and oversimplified. A more comprehensive approach incorporates the complexity of interrelated dynamics necessary to address root causes.[2]

In part, a search for predictability and the demand for decisive answers drive this tendency. I take a different approach. I believe that an emphasis on predictability and finding definitive answers often frustrates sustainable organizational change efforts because it tends to distort the complexity of organizational life. It breeds recommendations that respond more to symptoms than to root causes. It stifles the innovative approaches that would be more appropriate given the complexity of the situation.

Organizations are too complex for there to be one single approach or answer to understanding and addressing organizational challenges. The social processes of a group or organization are not static; they are always in flux as participants in the organization change, time passes, the environment shifts, and new technology is developed. Instead of one shared reality, organizational life is an ever-evolving assortment of socially constructed realities.

Reframing Professional and Disciplinary Boundaries

Organizations face challenges that are more complex than ever before. These challenges warrant, even necessitate, transdisciplinary, collaborative efforts. For example, to address environmental problems, people from diverse backgrounds, scientific disciplines, and responsibilities (e.g., regulatory agencies, biologists, marine biologists, climatologists, politicians, and indigenous people with generations of history working directly in the environment, such as crabbers and shrimpers if the issue relates to shrinking shellfish catches) must work together and share information and expertise. They must cooperate across political boundaries that the natural environment does not recognize; rivers and pollution do not adhere to county and state lines. This kind of work calls for collaboration and information sharing among people who may never have worked together; they might even be adversaries. They do not yet have a common language or the mutual trust that is required for substantive collaboration.

When parties to complex issues try to control the flow of information and knowledge, it suppresses spontaneity, learning, and knowledge creation as demonstrated by Brown and Duguid (1991, 2000), Nonaka (1994), and Wenger (1998). Thus, for proactive innovation, problem solving, and problem prevention, the boundaries and structures of knowledge need to be somewhat diffuse. Complex environments thrive on spontaneous, weblike networking connections that enable people to form ad hoc working groups and to be involved in multiple projects simultaneously. If expertise is too rigidly held in the silos of one discipline, one profession, or one country, the inroads to increased understanding and innovation are much more difficult to discover and are sometimes never found. Although norms must exist to guide the appropriate transmission of knowledge, organizations must share knowledge and information. When people are able to spontaneously seek each other out and follow their passion for problem solving, learning, and creativity, they begin to transform the walls of the silos into the more diffuse boundaries of flexible, adaptive environments.

People face challenges and opportunities as they strive to gain ready access to expertise from a myriad of interrelated arenas. How groups and organizations anticipate and meet challenges and opportunities depends in large measure on the nature and quality of their conversations, which are often the primary medium of organizational and interorganizational communication. Because all organizations are influenced by, and must interact with, their external environments, the intraorganizational and interorganizational dynamics further increase the demand for improved communication. Thus, there is a need for people to learn how to reframe their perceptions of disciplinary, professional, and national boundaries.

Enacting Organizations through Communication

People continuously make sense of their organizational environments (Boje 1991; Taylor 1999; Weick 1995). For instance, in our organizations we may notice decision-making patterns in terms of who is heard, who has access to information, what is encouraged and discouraged, and who is included or excluded. These observations of behavior shape how we make sense of organizational contexts.

Organizational life is not static. Instead, people *enact* their experiences in organizational settings through their everyday practices, conversations, and actions (Weick 1995). These complex webs of behaviors, actions, and conversations are never inert or isolated because they grow out of earlier individual and organizational experiences that in turn influence the present and future. People bring their unique histories into the mix. These histories range from recent interactions, such as those of a project team, to deeply ingrained assumptions and cultural norms about what behavior is appropriate or inappropriate and what will or will not work. Previous educational and professional training, work experiences, cultural backgrounds, and nationalities are examples of the conscious and unconscious influences that are continually affecting behavior.

For example, research and development (R&D) professionals will have different priorities and perspectives and will tell stories describing their work that are distinctly different from those told by a salesperson or the CEO of the same organization. Salespeople are likely to focus on sales quotas, dates for the debut of new services or products, and delivery times; they focus on short-term deliverables. R&D professionals typically emphasize less tangible factors and long-term goals as they conceptualize inventing new processes, services, or products. Focal points for the CEO would be the politics of working with board members, bottom-line financial issues, and long-term strategic goals.

In addition to the differing vantage points and priorities of the various parts of an organization, within each group individuals may have distinctly personal points of view. One sales manager might emphasize developing good relationships and offering prompt service to customers or clients. Another might stress competition among staff members to set and reach higher sales targets.

Thus, people interdependently act out, or enact, the actual life of any given organization through the roles they play (Figure 2.1). In addition, each organizational context has distinguishing characteristics that make prediction and generalization unreliable and essentially impossible. An organization's environment is not fixed. The actions that people take— and do not take—"create the materials that become the *constraints* and *opportunities* they face" (Weick 1995, 31) (emphasis added). In other words, perceptions about *constraints* and *opportunities* grow out of what has previously occurred, what is happening at a given moment in that setting, the individuals' histories and predispositions, and the organizational context.

Consider a hypothetical example: If employees notice that people

Figure 2.1   **Webs of organizational life**

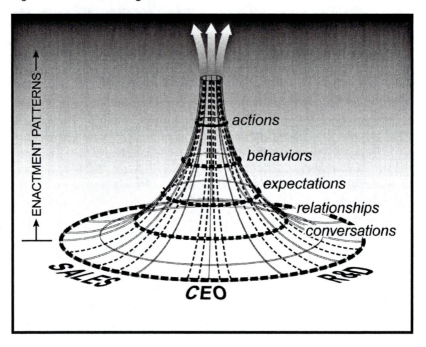

promoted into vacant positions always come from outside of their organization, they gradually begin to assume that promotions are unlikely for current
employees. Consciously or unconsciously, they are making sense of their
environment. If this pattern continues, people who stay in the organization
may operate according to the underlying assumptions of this perceived
constraint—that is, promotion is unlikely for them. They enact the pattern
either by staying with the organization and fundamentally accepting it or by
seeking opportunities to leave if promotion is a personal priority. Another
alternative is that an organizational change (i.e., promoting from within)
may break this pattern, thus setting new enactment patterns into motion.
Either way, people make sense of their surroundings through ongoing expectations, perceptions, conversations, relationships, action, and inaction.

Conversation as an Agent of Change

Through enactment, differing impressions and interpretations influence
whether subsequent conversations occur, how they develop, and who

the invited and uninvited participants are. Consequently, how people make sense of their interactions has implications for their capacity to listen and learn from each other and for organizations to change and be innovative.

If I have a conversation that strongly affirms the value of my input, it influences my expectations and probably my behavior in future conversations with the same people or in similar settings. The impressions and feelings that I have when a conversation is over have implications for what follows in subsequent conversations. These somewhat amorphous dimensions, such as impressions and feelings, affect future behavior as much as the words used.

In addition, the sense we make of any specific word may affect us differently depending on who says it or how they say it. Take for instance the word *courageous*. In a conversation reflecting on a recent meeting, suppose someone tells me that my behavior was courageous. I could take away the impression that the speaker admires me because I had the courage to speak up. However, by interpreting the word differently, I might take away the impression that the speaker sees me as naïve for not being more aware of the negative political risks of speaking up in this setting. My relationship with the speaker and other previous interactions affect this "sense-making."

How does enactment through conversation relate to change? The conceptual work of Ford and Ford (1995) highlights the centrality of conversation to organizational change. Other research on the topic tends to focus more on the actual words spoken and the assertive dimensions of speaking (Boje 1991; Ford 1999; Ford and Ford 1995; Habermas 1991). Ford and Ford (1995) propose that communication, and specifically conversation, is more focal than traditional organizational theories suggest, saying, "Change is a phenomenon that occurs within communication . . . we seek to firmly establish communication as the very medium within which change occurs" (p. 542). Thus, conversations and the sense made of them are the medium for change.

Ely and Meyerson (2000) similarly recognize the value of the "emergent, localized approach to . . . organizational change" (p. 142). Their research focuses on the manner in which gendering patterns in organizations can be changed, and is especially relevant here because it reinforces the relationship between conversations and substantial organizational change. They assume that people at least partially construct meaning through conversations and informal interactions in organizations. Accordingly, Ely and Meyerson (2000) suggest that through conversations people can critique and revise their perceptions of organizations, thereby making "it possible . . . to consider and experiment with new, previously inconceivable courses of action" (p. 135). Organizational conversations and time for reflection therefore are readily available mediums for this kind of critique and revision. Yet organizations often underestimate the value of reflection and conversation and thus waste these potential resources unless they make intentional efforts to use them constructively.

Catalytic Conversations that Invite Differences

Another aspect of organizational enactment is whether contrary ideas or opinions are encouraged or discouraged. If people who are working together consistently agree with each other and do not express divergent perspectives, the prevailing ideas and behaviors generally continue unquestioned. They become dominant assumptions and organizational norms and render contrary perceptions silent. The status quo remains more or less impervious to change. People slip into apathy or cynicism as they begin to assume that they have no capacity to influence change; or they slip into patterns of unexamined agreement, often referred to as *groupthink* or *attitude polarization* (Argyris 1997; Brodbeck et al. 2002; Janis 1972), and go along with prevailing ideas instead of rocking the boat. Intentionally or inadvertently, there is a silencing of alternative points of view. In either case, the organization does not receive the benefit of individual differences and differing resources of talent, expertise, experience, and wisdom that are resident within the organization remain dormant.

A particular disadvantage of this pattern is that the organization is vulnerable and misses early indications of impending changes both internally and with regard to the external environment. It fails to notice opportunities. As an example, Swiss watch companies that historically were the leaders in the industry were devastated because they failed to recognize that the future of timekeeping was in digital technology. At the same time, firms in Japan and Hong Kong captured much of the low- and mid-priced watch market segments (*Harvard Business Online* 2000). Failure to recognize early signs and anticipate market shifts from analog to digital timekeeping led to the demise of some Swiss businesses with long histories of success. In the organizations that missed these clues, their isolation from divergent perspectives and experience was a major reason that they lacked early evidence of the market shift to digital technology. Organizations that suppress divergent challenges to prevailing norms are distinctively vulnerable and may be victims of groupthink. Instead, open consideration of potential changes allows an organization to choose its future consciously rather than being blindsided and unprepared. Deliberate choices transform victims of groupthink into active participants who can more readily anticipate consequences and plan accordingly.

In organizational environments where people express divergent points of view and disagree, prevailing notions are open to question and new information. Especially if people disagree respectfully and try to speak in ways that are relatively easy to hear, their colleagues are more likely to reconsider the prevailing or dominant norms. The same colleagues will be better able to anticipate relevant impending business or political changes. The differences can become catalysts for reading internal and external environments, sharing expertise, creating new possibilities, and being more innovative (Alper and Tjosvold 1998; Eisenhardt, Kahwajy, and Bourgeois 1997).

Previous conversations can influence an individual's perception of whether or not colleagues will be receptive to unconventional suggestions. Because risk-taking behaviors are often associated with learning and innovation in organizations, these impressions potentially have wide rippling effects (Edmondson 1999). The surprise of hearing something that is unexpected can cause a shift in previously firm, even rigid, assumptions and positions. The surprise of difference provokes change that can lead to more fluid and dynamic conversations and relationships.

The nature of the change is pivotal. Lewin's work on organizational change as a sequence of unfreezing, moving, and refreezing patterns is a classic in the field of organizational studies (Lewin 1952; Schultz-Hardt, Jochims, and Frey 2002; Zand and Sorensen 1975). Although Lewin's work was groundbreaking in the 1940s, I propose that the idea of exchanging one rigid, frozen approach for another is problematic in contemporary organizations that are constantly functioning in a sea of change. If organizations refreeze (i.e., hold firmly in place) new approaches developed during a change process, ongoing learning that might contradict this new ideal is stifled. Refreezing inhibits flexibility, adaptation, and ongoing knowledge creation. Thus, if the change is not continuous, it leads to the reification of each new approach, leaving the organization as vulnerable in the end as it had been previously.

For example, suppose that the R&D arm of a large manufacturing corporation decides to set aside specific times for brainstorming to stimulate innovation. This change has the potential to increase the organization's ability to be ahead of competitors in developing new products or services and thus maintain or increase its market niche. As markets change, organizations on the cutting edge must continually embrace new kinds of expertise. As needed, the group may include new people with specific expertise, such as from information systems, in brainstorming sessions. At other gatherings, they may invite people with expertise in another area, such as nanotechnology, while sometimes bringing together a wide range of talent at the same time.

If, on the other hand, the organization is unable or unwilling to be flexible to these kinds of changes, the original change (i.e., designation of time for brainstorming) can become a hindrance to the organization if it reifies the underlying expectations about who has expertise, who is included, and when and how to brainstorm. Over time, the R&D group can become even more insular. In other words, if organizational changes result in new unbending norms, the inadvertent exclusion of differences in the form of new ideas, people, and expertise that is needed for next-generation products or services takes a toll.

In organizational studies, systemic change that has an impact on all parts of an organization is a common theme. The expectation is that what results from systemic change is therefore more likely to be sustainable over time. Instead, I propose seeking *generative change,* because it adds key dimensions. Not only does this type of change include self-generating aspects of sustainability, it also connotes life-giving qualities that stimulate relationships of trust and innovation.

It is important to note how catalytic conversations invite differences that both provoke and support generative change and new knowledge creation. Environments that are rich in generative change and creativity stimulate catalytic conversations, thereby creating mutually reinforcing processes. Figure 2.2 illustrates these complex processes.

These processes are not hierarchical or linear, but rather function as complex networks of influences. The quality of the work and relationships is heavily reflective of the quality of organizational communication. The chapters that follow elaborate on the separate elements of these dynamics and on the interactions among them.

Generative changes must be ongoing and be reinforced by an organization's cultural norms. A necessary warning here is that cultures typically change slowly, thus providing stability as well as inflexibility. Therefore, the organization must have "an ability to self-organize and regenerate

Figure 2.2   **"Magnetic field" of catalytic conversations**

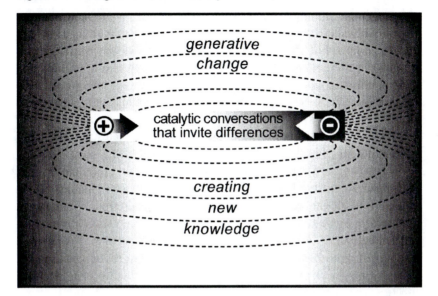

itself on a continuous basis . . . [making it essential] that the cultural codes uniting an organization foster an open and evolving approach to the future" (Morgan 2006, 97, 100). The norms must encourage ongoing generative change and wide-ranging influences.

The Power to Influence

Regardless of the source of a person's power, conversations are the primary medium of influence. Formally and informally, to accomplish the work of the organization people continuously organize and reorganize themselves through their conversations, connections, and relationships. In addition to designated leaders with formal roles of influence, informal leaders emerge. They do not have job descriptions or job titles that assign them positions of influence. Instead their influence emerges for a variety of reasons, including their frequent contact with key people, highly sought-after expertise, and personal charisma. As people come into and leave organizations, the formal leadership changes. Although informal relationships and networks also change, people with influence, regardless of their formal positions, provide continuity, pass on organizational wisdom and history, and thereby serve the organization in invaluable ways.

One implication is that people at all hierarchical and functional levels are able to influence changes. Yet the organizational receptiveness to influence from all levels affects whether responsibilities for generative change are widely dispersed throughout the organization. When influence is invited and welcomed, people tend to be more cognizant of the connections between their input and their self-interests. Nonetheless, responsibilities for final decision making also have to be clear. Organizations can still be decisive and proactive while integrating decentralized approaches and diverse input into decision-making processes. A key factor is the substantive integration of people into everyday practices of organizing rather than the assignment of input to discrete designated times.

I do not suggest that this approach is easy. The images and goals that guide this work are much more demanding than traditional management approaches (Amabile and Kramer 2007). Yet the contemporary world is in desperate need of generative change (Cook and Brown 1999; Frahm and Brown 2007). A high degree of intentionality is required. Neither catalytic conversations nor the goal for ongoing enhancement of organizational well-being is ordinary. Nor is the potential they offer.

In the next chapter, the complexity of these changes and the many considerations involved in the process are explored. The concepts and practicalities of self-organizing behaviors and emergent environments deepen insight into the meaning of ongoing generative change and knowledge creation.

Notes

1. The meaning of rational here is characteristic of positivist methodology and epistemological thinking. I elaborate further in Chapter 3.

2. The first limitation is characteristic of single-loop learning, while the second characterizes double-loop learning (Argyris 1997), which is discussed in Chapter 6.

References

Alper, S., and D. Tjosvold. 1998. Interdependence and controversy in group decision making: Antecedents to effective self-managing teams. *Organizational Behavior and Human Decision Processes* 74 (1): 33–52.

Amabile, T. M., and S. J. Kramer. 2007. Inner work life: Understanding the subtext of business performance. *Harvard Business Review* 85 (5): 72–83.

Argyris, C. 1997. *On organizational learning*. Malden, MA: Blackwell Publishers Inc.

Boje, D. M. 1991. The storytelling organization: a study of story performance in an office-supply firm. *Administrative Science Quarterly* 36: 106–126.

Brodbeck, F. C., R. Kerschreiter, A. Mojzisch, D. Frey, and S. Schutz-Hardt. 2002.

The dissemination of critical, unshared information in decision-making groups: The effects of pre-discussion dissent. *European Journal of Social Psychology* 32 (1): 35–56.

Brown, J. S. and P. Duguid. 1991. Organizational learning and communities-of-practice: Toward a unified view of working, learning and innovation. *Organization Science* 2 (1): 40–57.

Brown, J. S. and P. Duguid. 2000. *The social life of organization.* Boston: Harvard Business School Press.

Cook, S. D. N., and J. S. Brown. 1999. Bridging epistemologies: The generative dance between organizational knowledge and organizational knowing. *Organizational Science* 10 (4): 381–400.

Edmondson, A. 1999. Psychological safety and learning behavior. *Administrative Science Quarterly* 44: 350–383.

Eisenhardt, K. M., J. L. Kahwajy, and L. J. Bourgeois III. 1997. Conflict and strategic choice: How top management teams disagree. *California Management Review* 39 (2): 42–62.

Ely, R. J., and D. E. Meyerson. 2000. Theories of gender in organizations: A new approach to organizational analysis and change. In *Research in organizational behavior,* eds. B. M. Staw and R.I. Sutton, vol. 22. New York: Elsevier Science.

Ford, J. D. 1999. Organizational change as shifting conversations. *Journal of Organizational Change Management* 12 (6): 480–500.

Ford, J. D., and L. W. Ford. 1995. The role of conversations in producing intentional change in organizations. *Academy of Management Review* 20: 541–570.

Frahm, J., and K. Brown. 2007. First steps: Linking change communication to change receptivity. *Journal of Organizational Change Management* 20 (3): 370–387.

Habermas, J. 1991. *Moral consciousness and communicative action.* Cambridge, MA: The MIT Press.

Harvard Business Online. 2000. http://harvardbusinessonline.hbsp.harvard.edu/hbsp/index.jsp?_requestid=27930

Janis, I. L. 1972. *Victims of groupthink: A psychological study of foreign-policy decisions and fiascoes.* Boston: Houghton Mifflin Company.

Lewin, K. 1952. Group decision and social change. In *Readings in social psychology,* ed. G. E. Swanson and T. M. Newcomb. New York: Holt.

Morgan, G. 2006. *Images of organization.* Updated edition. Thousand Oaks, CA: Sage Publications.

Nonaka, I. 1994. A dynamic theory of organizational knowledge creation. *Organization Science* 5 (1): 14–37.

Schulz-Hardt, S., M. Jochims, and D. Frey. 2002. Productive conflict in group decision making: Genuine and contrived dissent as strategies to counteract biased information seeking. *Organizational Behavior and Human Decision Processes* 88 (2): 563–586.

Taylor, S. S. 1999. Making sense of revolutionary change: Differences in members' stories. *Journal of Organizational Change Management* 12 (6): 524.

Weick, K. E. 1995. *Sensemaking in organizations.* Thousand Oaks, CA: Sage.

Wenger, E. 1998. *Communities of practice: Learning, meaning, and identity.* New York: Cambridge University Press.

Zand, Dale E., and R. E. Sorensen. 1975. Theory of change and the effective use of management science. *Administrative Science Quarterly* 20 (December): 532–545.

3

Catalytic Conversations in Complex, Emergent Environments

Just as the importance of land in production changed dramatically as the economy moved from agriculture to industry, so too does the movement to a knowledge economy necessitate a rethinking of economic fundamentals. (Stiglitz 1999, 5)

Likewise, shifts to a knowledge economy necessitate a rethinking of organizational fundamentals. Organizational life has become too complex for a single individual, profession, or discipline to understand (Rycroft and Kash 1999). According to Price Pritchett, there was "more information produced in the last 30 years than in the previous 5,000, and the information supply available to us doubles every five years" (Tymon and Stumpt 2003, 12). Therefore, the changing faces of economics, trade, education, and government now require unprecedented demands for collaboration.

Traditional models of management and communication are inadequate in the face of such complexity. Many of the traditional models and tools important for organizational efficiency reflect worldviews and frames of reference that grew out of the Industrial Revolution. These same models now limit the imagination and constrain how much people can analyze and synthesize knowledge in order to comprehend complex phenomena or grasp them contextually. Complexity and emergence theories provide useful conceptual frameworks for describing and understanding these dynamic, changing phenomena.

Complex Environments

Organizations can seldom work effectively in isolation, and people in organizations likewise are rarely self-sufficient. Yet in the United States traditional models of leadership and reward structures focus largely on individuals. The incentive structures for most experts tend to reward individual accomplishment and the development of deeply specific disciplinary or professional expertise, rather than broad or cross-boundary experience and knowledge. Education and training for most experts, such as engineers or economists, are increasingly specialized and narrow. As the range of proficiency narrows, experts focus on ever smaller slices of organizational and societal life, thus distorting their perceptions of the expanding complexities. When experts collaborate with people who have different areas of expertise, backgrounds, and perspectives, their interactions can serve as catalysts to broaden perspectives beyond disciplinary boundaries.

When they engage in catalytic conversations, it becomes more likely that their communication will spur substantive new insights and collaborative interpretations of their complex surroundings. These interpretations in turn influence future actions and the interpretations of others. Work in complex environments thrives on the capacity for self-organization and emergent activities that grow out of interactions among people who work together and subsequently learn from their differences. People begin to *see* greater complexity and more possibilities as they collaborate with others and encounter differences in constructive environments.

Linear Thinking in Complex Environments

As study and management of organizations emerged over the second half of the twentieth century, they incorporated the prevailing rational and positivist research methodologies from other disciplines at that time, which in turn shaped theory and practice in these fields. Using those models, popular problem-solving strategies use analytical processes that break large problems into small pieces rather than synthesizing approaches that incorporate the complexity and consider contextual implications. Operating upon the assumption that it is possible to study isolated segments without distorting the data and results, these researchers tend to segment problems. These models are used to identify definable cause-and-effect, i.e., linear, relationships, that can in turn be used for prediction and control (see Figure 3.1).

Yet given the multitude of overlapping and conflicting demands, influences, cultures, priorities, and interests at play within organizations and society, linear thinking that seeks to find one or a few causes to a

Figure 3.1   **Problem-solving strategy in different environments**

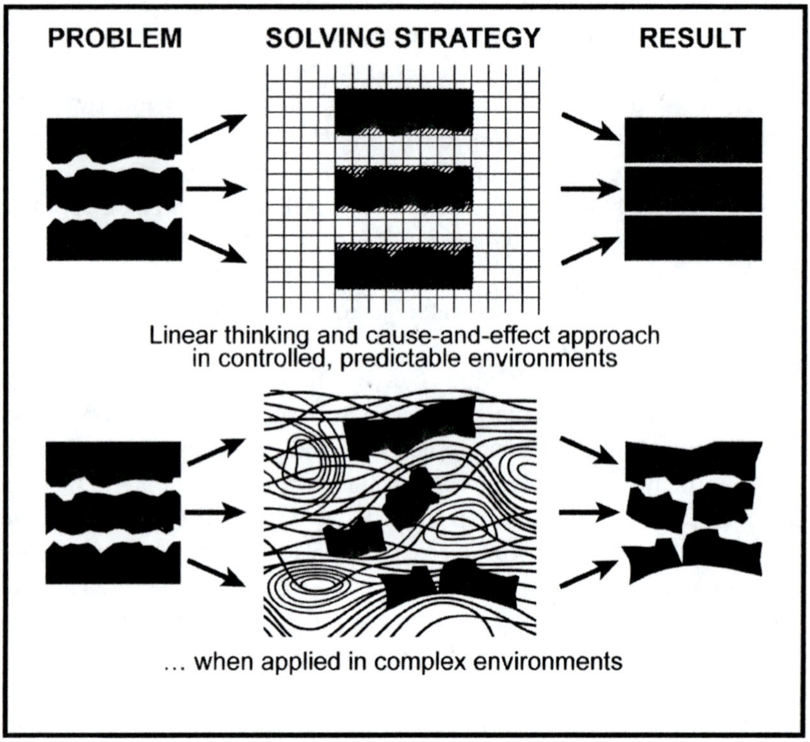

PROBLEM   SOLVING STRATEGY   RESULT

Linear thinking and cause-and-effect approach
in controlled, predictable environments

... when applied in complex environments

problem is inadequate except in limited situations, such as routine or highly predictable situations. Because this approach can give the illusion of predictability and control, it can actually exacerbate problems, as reflected in Figure 3.1. This phenomenon is especially inadequate for understanding complex human behavior and relations. As collections of widely diverse people interact, the complexity increases exponentially, thus making organizational life even more complicated. Almost as many interpretations of what is going on in a given setting exist as there are participants. For many organizational challenges, linear thinking and cause-and-effect problem solving blind participants from perceiving and understanding critical parts of problems. Isolating a few aspects of a situation to diagnose what are, in fact, intricate and complicated interorganizational problems is as inadequate as a medical doctor treating symptoms without diagnosing the underlying disease. Without trying to get a better grasp of the whole problem, progress will always be limited by the parts of the picture that we cannot—or will not—see.

To illustrate the limitations of linear thinking and problem solving, a hypothetical example of a common occurrence may be helpful. The setting is a midsize organization facing a crisis. There are approximately 350 employees. The four individuals in the top management team generally work well together. The team meets as soon as a crisis becomes clearly apparent. They consider a variety of possible approaches to the problems, take several weeks to gather data to help them in their decision making, report their results to one another, and develop a clear strategy to move the organization through the crisis to a healthier future.

Their next step is to bring the organization's middle managers into the process. At a meeting with these managers, the management team outlines the crisis and the strategy that it developed in response. Management team members charge the middle managers with passing the plan throughout the organization and to begin implementation as soon as possible. On the surface, this approach has merit. We see a group of leaders who can work together effectively; are willing to confront the crisis, gather data, and talk about various options; and are decisive. Bright people who know their organization well have developed the plan. What could be missing?

First, leaders cannot know or understand enough of the wealth of organizational experience, tacit knowledge, or complexity of dynamics residing there to embark on such major change without tapping those resources. People throughout the organization who collectively have that experience and knowledge accomplish their work through formal and informal networks, routines, relationships, conversations, and ways of adapting to challenges on a daily, if not hourly, basis. Even if one or more members of the team talked to other employees during the few weeks of data collection, such contacts are often uneven, fail to represent the diversity of the organization, and, with rare exceptions, probably left out the people most likely to be affected.

The second problem with this linear, top-down strategy developed by only four people is that there is limited consideration of the complex implications for several hundred employees. The implementation of the plan is likely to affect almost everyone in the organization and many external stakeholders. When the organizational employees hear about the final plan that they must implement, they are likely to feel confused, unappreciated, dismissed, and unacknowledged. Frustration builds when they have information that contradicts assumptions made by the leaders. Apprehension and feelings of vulnerability come with organizational change, yet the plan does not consider these concerns or how to address them.

A third problem is that the team does not consider how employees would learn about, or interpret, the new plan. Some people will hear about it earlier than others, setting off a rash of informal communication and rumors resulting in little uniformity among the actual messages received by employees. No plan is in place for how to keep employees informed over time.

Even if the middle managers and the leadership team try to give participants opportunities for bottom-up input and then try to incorporate it, the organization has lost precious time by not being more inclusive from the beginning. Delays in response to the crisis are almost inevitable. Many of the organization's most valued employees will be reticent at best to devote their time and talent heartily to the plan. Some employees are likely to do even more damage to the organization if they are openly critical of the leadership team's actions.

As in this case, when an issue perceived as a problem emerges in an organization, it is common to shift into a top-down, problem-solving mode. Yet the more predisposed an organization is to using linear approaches, the stronger the tendency is to fail to address underlying complex organizational dynamics and innovative alternatives. I propose using these concepts to create new ways of conceptualizing organizational dynamics.

Complexity and Chaos

Modern physics has influenced all aspects of life in knowledge-intensive economies. Its influence extends beyond technology to "the realm of thought and culture where it has led to a deep revision in our conception of the universe and our relation to it" (Capra 1991, 17). In the 1980s a group of eclectic scientists from diverse disciplines recognized that many contemporary challenges are far too complex to address without pushing into new paradigms. This group founded the Santa Fe Institute.

George Cowan, one of the founders of the institute, wrote, "The moment you depart from the *linear approximation,* you're navigating on a very broad ocean" (emphasis added) (as quoted in Waldrop 1992, 66). Cowan's metaphor articulates the chasm that must be traversed to move from linearity to the ambiguity embedded in complex systems. Relinquishing what Cowan calls the "linear approximation" can shake the stability of our understanding of how the world works, that is, our worldviews. Yet to accomplish sustainable organizational change, leaders must be open to complexity and learn how to navigate that "broad ocean." Accomplishing this kind of change is an ongoing journey, not a destination or a goal, and calls for an inexhaustible openness to learning and willingness to accept outside influences.

Increasing knowledge about complexity and chaos grows out of quantum physics as it emerged in the twentieth century. This new work on complex systems attempts "to uncover and understand the deep commonalities that link artificial, human, and natural systems" (Santa Fe Institute 2009). Stuart Kauffman describes complexity as "a natural expression of a universe that is not in equilibrium . . . differences, potentials, drive the formation of complexity" (1995, 19). Waldrop uses simple and direct language to describe his meaning of *complexity* by saying that it is where a "great many independent agents are interacting with each other in a great many ways" (1992, 11).

Certainly, the complexity of differences and the value of opening ourselves to learning through encountering differences create disequilibrium. At the same time, embedded in the interactions and catalytic conversations among people with diverse expertise is the potential for innovation (Bijlsma-Frankema, Rosendaal, and Taminiau 2006). People in the most innovative organizations form and work in communities of practice or other kinds of highly creative and dynamic environments that serve both the organization and people well (Wenger 1998).

There is further complexity in organizational dynamics, given that organizational stakeholders have shared interests and yet also represent differing constituencies, many of which are external to an organization. As an illustration of complex *inter*organizational dynamics, let's look at a proposed coastal land development project that I worked on early in my career as a coastal zone management planner. One of my responsibilities was to study the proposed project, work with the stakeholders, and make recommendations for the approval or disapproval of the required permits to build in or near a coastal wetland area.

Stakeholders for this project included investors of a development company, current residents who lived in proximity to the proposed changes, the chamber of commerce and several economic development groups representing business interests, numerous environmental groups, elected state and local officials, agencies responsible for providing the infrastructure to support the development (e.g., water and sewer districts, power companies, highway departments, and school districts), governmental regulatory interests, and various academics with related research interests among others.

Many of the stakeholder groups—if not all—shared at least an understanding of the need for or a desire for economic benefit for the community. Yet the groups' priorities varied greatly. On the surface, people in each category, such as residents, played distinct roles. However, people within each group were not homogeneous, thus creating subtle and not-so-subtle intragroup dynamics that further tangled the web of complexity set in motion when national, state, local, economic, and environmental interests competed with each other.

Individuals and stakeholder groups wore multiple hats. Among the residents or owners of property in the affected areas were people who did not want their community developed, others who wanted to sell their property at a profit, and some who had strong animosity toward regulatory agencies. Simultaneously, the constituents of the state and local officials included some of these diverse affected residents as well as environmentalists and pro-development interests, all of whom exerted considerable conflicting pressure on these decision makers and on residents. Past and future campaign contributors, upon whom these officials depended, included individuals and companies who often were influential voices in these diverse groups.

As if these conflicting pressures were not enough, the process over time continually changed during the several years of the controversy. At various specific points in the process, the accounts of individuals and groups of the events sounded irrational and unrecognizable when compared to the others. At different stages in the conflict as the situation progressed, the descriptions and stories changed. These differences are a good example of what Patricia Shaw (2002) meant, saying that " . . . complexity is created by the fact that all the agents are responding to one another's signals all the time in an iterative, non-linear dynamic" (p. 66). These iterative processes become convoluted and unpredictable as pressures from opposing points of view mount.

In this case, endless conversations took place and relationships were negotiated and renegotiated as coalitions emerged and evolved, contributing even further to the complexity. Some of the parties involved shifted their positions as a result of these ongoing negotiations, which created an evolving landscape of alliances. Shaw (2002) offers an astute description of how this kind of complexity gets played out in conversations over time.

> From within the conduct of the conversation, what seems solid would be melting at the edges, while what seems shapeless would be gaining form, at the same time, not to create a single unified landscape for all, but a shifting topology of partial orderings in which we recreate our situation as both recognizable and potentially novel at the same time. (p. 68)

In these kinds of situations, as people have influence and are influenced by others, the *solid edges* of their highly polarized positions can begin to either *melt* or become more hardened. Alternatives emerge that were unimagined early in the dispute. If alternatives develop as conversations take place, they give *form* over time to what had been *shapeless*. As people talk and begin to understand each other better, the positions that they take may soften and bleed into each other a bit, almost as if the *topology* of the *landscape* is *shifting*. The movement at times can seem painfully slow, while at other times it feels more like an avalanche. Rarely is a *single unified landscape* created where everyone agrees on how to proceed with a project. Over time decisions and plans can emerge from earlier conversations that are *recognizable* and *novel at the same time.* When these creative alternatives emerge, we can say that people are working together in the *zone of complexity at the edge of chaos.*

In this case early in my professional career, I wish I had had the benefit of experience and research I have gained over the years. On the other hand, my participation in and observation of the productive and counterproductive conversations and negotiations in this case influenced my research and learning. I sought to discover more constructive ways for people to interact and use their differences as resources to find innovative alternatives to the compromises that characterized the outcomes of this case—compromises that left most parties less than satisfied with the outcome.

The Edge of Chaos

As Kauffman (1995) suggests, complexity is an unavoidable expression of natural interactions. By drawing upon *complexity sciences,* one way to understand these interactions is along a continuum from rigid order to utter chaos, a range that can represent human behavior and organi-

Figure 3.2 **The zone of complexity at the edge of chaos**

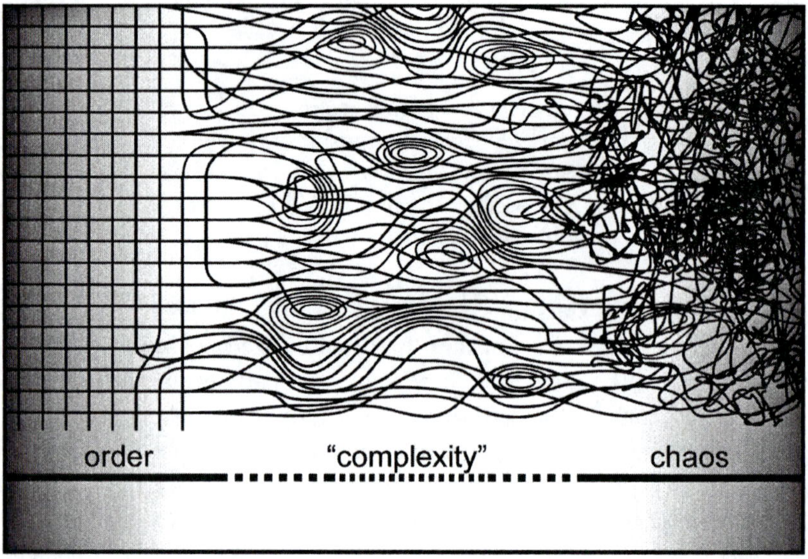

order   "complexity"   chaos

zational dynamics. In complex systems, there are strong attractions in dialectically opposing directions (Capra 1991, 1982).

For example, within one organization there might be groups that tend to be orderly in their deliberations and others that tend to be more chaotic. Or the pace of work for a group may vary erratically from day to day or from one time of the year to another because of seasonal demands—such as a certified public accountant in the months before taxes are due. The tension between the strong pull toward order and its opposing extreme, chaos, collides at a midpoint called the *edge of chaos*. Figure 3.2 illustrates this delicate middle zone.

When there is not enough tension between the two extremes and when differences between people do not surface, order tends to take over and the system or organization can become stagnant, dull, and rigid. On the other hand, if the attractions in the other direction become too strong, chaos and anarchy reign.

Order at the far left end of the diagram in Figure 3.2 represents the perpetuation of the "modus operandi" and an "all is well" mind-set. At its extreme, we can think of it as tightly wired as in Figure 3.2 or as solid, unmovable blocks of ice. In organizational life, people manifest this extreme when they try to control or establish predictability through elaborate rules and procedures in bureaucracies, autocratic top-down management, and other inflexible hierarchies. The efforts to control and predict typically include the suppression of disagreement and the encouragement of conformity (Argyris 1997), that is, the antithesis of catalytic conversations, which bring disagreements to the surface.

As organizations move away from the far left of the continuum of order, flexibility increases as people are more able to self-organize and try new ideas. They move away from the maintenance of order and enter the transitional zone of complexity (the edge of chaos). This edge of chaos can be compared to a pot of boiling water; the surface of the water is like a thin edge of chaos as it evaporates and changes into vaporlike steam (Waldrop 1992). Similarly, the members of a team engaged in catalytic conversations intensively, yet respectfully, surface their differences and strive to create innovative alternatives (Bijlsma-Frankema et al., 2006).

At the opposite end of the continuum, far away from order, is chaos, where there is no rhyme or reason to what is happening. Everything is erratic and discontinuous. It is as if the solid ice melted and became water that evaporates into gaseous turbulence. In chaotic organizations, people have no sense of what they should be doing or how their roles fit into broader goals or purposes. Their positions seem to be extremely precarious. Their work lives are constantly changing and they have no control over what occurs. They consider changes and management decisions to be irrational. They can be verbally abused without the respect and discipline of constructive disagreement and catalytic conversations present in the transitional zone at the edge of chaos.

Chaotic systems are overtaken by "weirdly unpredictable gyrations" that "dissolve into turbulence" (Waldrop 1992, 12). Waldrop's example of an organizational context that has become chaotic is one in which people do not know what they are supposed to do; they work at cross purposes. According to chaos theory, very small changes are amplified into unpredictable, widespread effects in the system (Kauffman 1995; Waldrop 1992). A frequently cited example is of a butterfly that flaps its wings in one part of the world, setting off a series of changes that ultimately affect weather in distant regions.

Working at the Edge of Chaos

Let's explore a simple organizational example of managing in this transitional zone in a marketing department. The director allocates substantial new resources to a project team charged with developing a highly innovative marketing plan for a new project. The director assures the team of her support and guidance as long as it stays within the allocated resources and other broad parameters that she establishes, such as a timeline, budget, and quality criteria. As the team begins work, the team members move into the transitional zone. If they need guidance, the director is available, although she does not intrude or micromanage. If the team ignores the parameters or takes extreme risks, it is likely to slip into chaos. If it focuses on establishing rigid rules and protocols for the work, it slips out of the middle and into order.

To operate at the edge of chaos, organizations such as this marketing department need to set clear parameters for quality control within which people have considerable flexibility to adapt and be innovative. Such organizations encourage and support people who try new approaches and take risks partially through previously developed relationships of trust and by not punishing well-intentioned failure.

At the edge of chaos,

> . . . the components of a system never quite lock into place, and yet never quite dissolve into turbulence . . . [it is] where life has enough stability . . . and enough creativity . . . where new ideas and innovative genotypes are forever nibbling away at the edges of the status quo. (Waldrop 1992, 12)

By working in this transitional zone, organizations often find the most potent opportunities for generative change and knowledge creation even though life at the edge of chaos is ambiguous and unpredictable. It involves living within the tension that exists between the strong attractions toward opposite poles. Phil Slater described it as "hovering delicately in the spaces between things" (Hampden-Turner 1994, xvii). This space, which can nourish new possibilities, is unstable. Underestimating the interdependencies of complex influences in organizations can drive team members into chaos. Accumulation of rapid changes without adequate preparation and support can tip an organization over the edge.

When trying to work in this zone, the only way to avoid slipping into chaos or retreating into the familiarity of order and stability is through deliberate *intentionality*. To take advantage of the potential of this fragile zone, people must have enough support to take risks, build trusting relationships, listen to learn, create opportunities for reflection, and learn from their differences. Catalytic conversations offer a medium that facilitates working at the edge of chaos. It does not mean pulling away all forms of structure, however, because that would push people into bewildering places where they would not know the source of decision making or funding, for example. Subsequent chapters will explore ways to provide necessary support while straddling the thin lines of distinction between order and chaos.

The coastal zone land development project mentioned earlier can serve as an example of working, or not working, at the edge of chaos. One option in a stalemate of such a project would be for the parties to enter negotiation or mediation, in which decisions are still in the hands of the parties rather than an outside arbitrator or a judge in an ensuing lawsuit. People are often reluctant to enter mediation because it is unfamiliar to them or because the outcomes on the front end are unclear and risky. By entering into any formal negotiations, the possibility for beneficial, *win-win* outcomes is an option. Yet without skillful and neutral mediators, the possibility of a *win-lose* outcome may be more likely. There is also the possibility that the negotiations will fail or a key party might disclose through the mediation potentially damaging information if there is a stalemate or lawsuit. However, prenegotiated agreements can minimize the disclosure issue. Much depends on the nature of the negotiations.

In this case example, there were no mediations or skilled negotiators with enough status and credibility to engage key stakeholders in such efforts. The outcome of the case was a limited development that brought less economic benefit to the developer and the community than planned as well as changes that deteriorated the environment and the integrity of the community. Unwillingness or lack of awareness about working at the edge of chaos resulted in compromises rather than innovative alternatives.

Another alternative to mediation that is a less risky and less public approach is to enter behind-the-scenes negotiations where efforts are out of the spotlight. In such cases, more mutually successful outcomes and innovative alternatives can emerge. When intra- and interorganizational dynamics are flexible enough for people to engage in adaptive, self-organizing behaviors, substantial changes can occur. Alternatives are discovered through catalytic conversations that uncover new information. For example, in another of my cases at the coastal agency, through informal, yet circumscribed negotiations, the parties learned that adjacent landowners could be persuaded to sell their property to allow for the relocation of the proposed development to a less environmentally fragile part of the coast.

A macrolevel example is the airline industry in the United States in the 1970s and 1980s. Prior to the late 1970s, airline companies had operated for many years under the relative protection and predictability of government regulation. When the industry was deregulated, the airlines were suddenly in a state of flux, bordering on chaos. Overnight the industry had to compete in an open market. The pressures for cultural change within these organizations called upon people to adapt rapidly to substantially different ways of doing business.

Highly regulated industries operate according to strict procedures. The regulation provides stability and more predictability than the open market can. Often companies in regulated industries have hierarchical reporting patterns that limit multidirectional and open communication. Shifting out of such a bureaucratic structure and mindset is extremely difficult. However, by altering patterns of interaction, shifts can occur. Innovation and entrepreneurship within the organization must be encouraged and rewarded. One approach is to involve people at all levels in sessions, guided by trained facilitators, to gather their input and ideas for changes. The purposes of the sessions include allowing people to express their hopes and concerns, brainstorm ideas, communicate the benefits and needs for change, build trust, and develop interim measures to ameliorate the natural fear of dramatic change; encouraging relationships to develop; and providing opportunities for people to learn from one another. Developing the ability to operate within a transitional region, (i. e., the edge of chaos) is essential. When the modus operandi in a company is too rigid and the demands for finite planning and prediction are too strong, innovation is stifled and it is difficult to create alternatives and new agreements. The decline of the organization is thus set in motion.

Considering When and How to Work at the Edge of Chaos

Because organizational life is socially constructed, each context and local situation is different to some degree. People's behavior originates at the local, interpersonal level and "what is learned is in part unique to those involved because it is based on previous accumulated learning that is partly tacit" (Rycroft and Kash 1999, 11). Whether, when, and how to work at the edge of chaos depends on context; and living and working in this unstable environment is not always possible or desirable. For example, in crises such as fires or accidents with serious injuries, strict orderly procedures are necessary to facilitate quick, effective, and potentially lifesaving responses. Firefighters and emergency medical personnel must know how to respond quickly in a wide variety of situations. At the other extreme, orderly environments may be ideal for simple, repetitive tasks.

Even in organizations that thrive in the transitional zone, people need to take breaks from the intensity. They need periods of calm to rest, reflect, and restore, which are designed specifically to slow the pace. For instance, participants in fast-paced entrepreneurial organizations need to have flexible work patterns, opportunities for rest, regular off-site retreats, time for individual and collective reflection, and opportunities to nurture relationships.

When working in organizations where change is essential and *all is not well,* people need support and flexibility to learn how to adapt to working in the delicate transitional middle region. Collaboration and open communication are keys to working effectively in transitional regions and discovering inspired alternatives. People who will be affected by upcoming changes need to be a part of the process, especially when they are not the main decision makers. People must be able to sustain openness to change and should be given additional space, technology, and support.

Even when people want change, reservations and resistance crop up. Participants may feel reluctant or afraid to take risks and unconsciously fashion barriers to the changes in an effort to preserve some semblance of stability. They may fear that projects they value are in jeopardy, that their roles in the organization will be undermined, or that current funding sources will disappear. Open access to communication—e.g., brainstorming, support groups, information sessions, and scenario building—help them get enough support to diminish fears and make changes seem less risky. Without careful preparation and cultivation of readiness for change, movement is likely to be stymied (Argyris 1997; Block 2000). If changes are too extreme and too fast, organizations and work groups are likely to either become increasingly resistant to change or slip into chaos.

In both the natural and social worlds, complex influences put stress on existing systems and lead to random interactions. As these random interactions begin to coalesce into decipherable patterns, new *self-organizing* behaviors develop and become recognizable, especially initially, among people in conversations. For example, ad hoc groups emerge to create a new product, service, or market. Entrepreneurs discover opportunities with colleagues that they pursue together. Like-minded people talk about their concerns or hopes and form coalitions to build new initiatives or to increase their influence.

Self-organizing Behaviors

As the world changed over the last half of the twentieth century, people needed more than ever to understand complex patterns of interdependencies and often found that the national borders and boundaries of traditional disciplines stood in the way. As new knowledge and technology were created faster than ever, many people in research and education were delving into deeper and narrower fields. I repeat some of these phenomena because they are so fundamental to understanding self-organizing patterns. As the practical need to push across disciplinary boundaries increased, most trends in education, technical training, and research were moving in opposite directions toward increasing specialization. As the economic and political needs to work across national boundaries increased, more adversarial relationships developed in many parts of the world.

Cambray (2002) describes the importance of bridging traditional separations to address the challenges in contemporary societies:

> Since the 1970s, a new paradigm cutting across scientific disciplines has been gaining attention; it focuses on the ways in which the order and organization of various systems spanning micro- and macro-worlds— [such as] chemical reactions, the weather, ecosystems, socio-political events, economics, trends, and so on—can arise spontaneously out of chaotic conditions through processes of *self-organization.* (emphasis added) (p. 414)

Social and political policies ultimately influence chemical and molecular reactions in nature in ways that influence weather and the environment as a whole. Economic policies and sociopolitical events have profound impacts on international trade and ecosystem dynamics. Each of the worlds in Cambray's examples is born out of tensions between the micro and macro; that is, the local and global or the interpersonal and organizational. Similar tensions operate between order and chaos and between pattern and surprise.

An organization's policies and its culture influence communication patterns (such as who has access to information, who has influence, and timeliness of information transmission). At the same time, people's expectations and behavior inside of organizations shape the policies and culture. When an organization's work requires employee initiatives and collaboration and when employees are entrepreneurial, leadership gets pressure to open communication and provide flexibility. These pressures in turn shape policies as well as the social and cultural norms. Working across the macro/micro boundaries is yet another form of maneuvering at the edge of chaos. It means appreciating the range of influences along the broad continua without choosing one approach at the expense of the other. Complex problems, for instance, demand that people pay attention to both micro and macrolevel influences to understand the issues, increase effectiveness, and affect change.

The global energy crisis is an example of the need for self-organizing groups to cross the boundaries of disciplines. Using the expertise of scholars or practitioners of geology, engineering, physics, or any of the physical sciences alone will not solve the energy crisis. Addressing the energy crisis without also recognizing the roles of public policy and human behavior is as inadequate as trying to solve world hunger by growing more food with no consideration for distribution patterns to get food to the people who most need it.

In complex environments, organizations must be able to access expertise both within and outside of their organizations to be innovative. People must be able to self-organize across traditional boundaries such as professional backgrounds, job titles, or level in the hierarchy. Competition in hiring and the changing demographics of employees also puts pressure on organizations to enhance work environments.

> [Given the shift away from] efficient management of mass markets and tangible assets to innovation and the effective utilization of knowledge and human capital resources, organizations and their leaders must also change. . . . Rather . . . firms must increasingly rely on the knowledge, skills, experience, and judgment of all their people. The entire organization collectively must create and assimilate new knowledge, encourage innovation, and learn to compete in new ways in an ever-changing competitive environment. (Dess and Picken 2000, 18)

Running counter to trends toward specialization, people increasingly recognize the need for self-organizing boundary-crossing patterns. The search to understand a "common theoretical framework for complexity that would illuminate nature and humankind" (Waldrop 1992, 12) led to the founding of the Santa Fe Institute, as mentioned earlier. In addition, over the last quarter of the twentieth century, programs and institutes of interdisciplinary studies cropped up on many college and university campuses. New disciplines emerged, such as organizational studies, organizational learning, knowledge management, and environmental sciences, in the search to understand more about the complex dilemmas faced by society. Matrix and cross-functional teams surfaced in the corporate and public worlds to provide organizations with easier access to their in-house expertise that was scattered across separate departments or divisions. To make it easier for organizations to access their widely distributed, previously nonintegrated knowledge, these teams were created. There are two common denominators that cut across these diverse trends (i.e., an increased awareness of self-organizing groups and emergent behaviors).

People bound by inflexible organizational structures are unable to respond quickly, talk to people as needed, or work effectively in complex, unpredictable, and ambiguous situations. When power is rigidly concentrated in hierarchies, it stifles exploration into unknown or less well-known areas to create new knowledge (Brown and Duguid 2000; Nonaka 1994; Wenger 1998). In the face of crises such as mergers and downsizings, a common response is for managers to increase their control. They restrict the flow of information about unclear impending changes and rigidly enforce existing procedures. As employees or customers require more information in the face of uncertainty, authoritative or valid information becomes more scarce.

Managers may block information flow because they do not have a lot of information, because legal counsel advises them not to share the information, or because they cannot predict outcomes. They pull back on their internal communication at the very time that their employees need to know what is happening. Rarely do they say, "I do not know," which can open the door for new learning (Bennis 2003). They do not realize how much it can help employees to hear leadership acknowledge that they do not have all the answers, they understand that waiting is harrowing, and they will share information as soon as they can.

Without a communication plan to help them through the crises, people access internal and external relationships and networks for information. As the organization tries to suppress the flow of information and communication, informal networks generate off-the-record gossip, and storytelling flourishes. To find out what is going on and cope with the uncertainty, self-organizing groups emerge. People may form new alliances and rumors grow rapidly as people share bits of information. As they speculate, the collective imagination grows. Fragments of conversations, bits of incidents, and versions of stories spread rapidly to fill the vacuum created by the excessive control of top-down managers.

This gossip and speculation may be wildly incorrect and counterproductive for management and for the organization. If management keeps the lines of communication open, it can somewhat diffuse these tendencies. At the very least, management can clarify what is misinformation and acknowledge what is unknown. Management also can allow people to talk about their concerns in carefully facilitated sessions that do not degenerate into negativity. Leaders need strong communication skills and good professional facilitators to handle these tense situations.

The capacity for continuous learning is pivotal. "As much as 70 to 80 percent of economic growth is now said to be due to new and better knowledge" (Joint Research Centre of the European Commission 2000). For people to learn and benefit from these rapid changes, they need to have ready access to information and feedback that is flowing throughout the organization and have flexibility to adapt to highly ambiguous environments (Hislop 2002). Rycroft and Kash's research (1999) and the subsequent case studies they have developed from various cultures are relevant here. Rycroft and Kash focused on learning about organizations in which complex technological innovation thrives. They found that "organizations that become proficient at monitoring and acting upon the rapid and complex flow of information are the most successful in reforming themselves—by self-organization . . . [which is] dependent upon and central to a continuing learning process" (p. 62). Their work and many other studies emphasize the importance of knowledge sharing for innovation (Choi, Kang, and Lee 2008; Kim and Lee 2006).

Key components of continuous learning include an organization's ability to scan its environments and use information proactively. Perhaps even more valuable is the organization's capacity to *remember* and learn from experience as it goes through crises. In other words, they need to know how to engage in catalytic conversations. People must continue to learn, remain in the organization so the organization can benefit from the accumulated knowledge, and share what they know with each other. Through this learning, people can better anticipate changes, increase their capacity for proactive behavior, and have a better chance of using what they have learned to benefit the organization. Sustainable, generative organizational change depends on this kind of organizational learning and organizational memory.

When communication and feedback are blocked or only flow in one direction, such as top-down from managers to employees, learning and subsequent innovation is inhibited. Rigid reporting structures block learning. Laying off people or otherwise allowing the ones with years of tacit organizational knowledge to walk out of the door drains organizational resources. The need for more information is exacerbated. If, on the other hand, communication and feedback flow freely, people can engage in catalytic conversations and readily learn from each other. By sharing information they are more likely to work collaboratively, form ad hoc groups to address complex issues, and be innovative. These kinds of self-organizing behaviors set the stage for emergent behaviors.

Emergent Theory and Behaviors

The last few decades are an example of what Talcott Parsons (1937) called *theoretical convergence*. There are times when in essence similar theories of action *emerge* in unexpectedly diverse places. The increased interest in emergence theory across quite diverse disciplines exemplifies Parsons's description of convergence of theories (Ali and Zimmer 1997; Sawyer 2002).

Self-organizing behaviors are at the core of adaptation. They grow out of the pressures for change and innovation in the natural and the social world. When self-organizing groups have ready access to multidirectional feedback, they are more likely to adapt and be *emergent* (Hislop 2002). In emergent organizations, "complex systems generate new properties . . . that form and interact in new ways or manifest new behaviors" (Rycroft and Kash 1999, 260). In other words, the organizational culture not only allows, but encourages adaptation. Emergent behaviors are not random. They have a focus and an enhancing effect. Because scientists and researchers now know more about how complex systems adapt, the emphasis is currently on trying to *create* emergence. Johnson (2001) describes this dynamic as channeling creative energy "toward specific forms for it to blossom into something like intelligence" (p. 119).

Johnson (2001) explains further as follows:

Figure 3.3   **Spiral of creating the conditions**

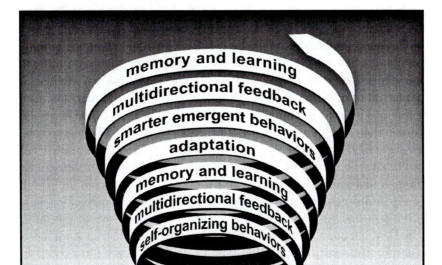

Emergent complexity without adaptation is like the intricate crystals formed by a snowflake: It's a beautiful pattern, but it has no function. The forms of emergent behavior [of interest here] show the distinctive quality of *growing smarter over time,* and of responding to the specific and changing needs of their environment. . . .
(emphasis added) (p. 20)

Although complex, the snowflake is not capable of adapting, learning, or growing smarter. By learning more about emergent entities that adapt, change, and learn, it is possible for organizations to focus more attention on microlevel communication, which is often a source of adaptation. To illustrate, Figure 3.3 shows the overlapping processes of growing smarter. The upwardly spiraling cycles illustrate emergent behavior over time.

Rycroft and Kash (1999) give us insight into what enables highly innovative organizations working with complex technologies to be cauldrons of continuous learning, emergence, and innovation. "Central to the notion of emergence is the fact that complex networks are not always created either as a function of selection by environmental forces or conscious choices by network members. *Complex network organizations are continually emerging* . . . innovative organizations . . . are always in the process of becoming rather than ever reaching equilibrium" (pp. 66–67). The work of continual emergence and the process of becoming is a prime example of working at the edge of chaos. Rather than trying to identify causal links or trying to make organizations continuously innovate, the challenge is in *creating conditions* that encourage and support adaptation and emergence.

One key element in *intentionally* creating such necessary conditions is to recognize the potential of using conversations as a primary medium for adaptation and emergence. The bottom-up feedback and the possibilities for adapting, changing, and learning are dynamic processes that are continuously unfolding, becoming, and evolving. Because feedback can provoke new ideas in unimagined directions, in feedback-rich environments these recurring patterns can be especially unpredictable. The environment does not produce an immediate result as much as encourage the cyclical interactions of feedback, memory, and learning (Johnson 2001; Beeson and Davis 2000; Rycroft and Kash 1999). Catalytic conversations activate the environment by promoting the exploration of differences. Flexibility, reflection, and a tolerance for ambiguity encourage cycles of emergent behaviors that extend generative change (Beeson and Davis 2000; Orlikowski 2002).

With these changes comes a challenge to walk the fine line between allowing the spontaneity for people to self-organize and providing enough organizational structure to avoid slipping into chaos. By offering enough structure to channel these behaviors, continuous learning and smarter explorations can drive emergence. It is essential to provide "'organization-wide' enabling conditions that promote a more favorable climate for effective knowledge creation" (Nonaka 1994, 27). Even though " . . . ideas are formed in minds of individuals, interaction between individuals typically plays a critical role in developing these ideas" (p. 15).

By understanding more about the conditions that encourage collaborative creation of new knowledge and innovation, we are more able to foster such favorable climates. With conscious intentions, receptive and inviting environments can be created to support emergent behaviors in organizations that are flatter and more flexible rather than in those with unbending hierarchies and rigid control. Environments that encourage and support spontaneous interactions, risk taking, organizational learning, relationship building, and multidirectional feedback provide superb settings for self-organizing entities to ripen and flourish.

> A learning organization is skilled at developing, accumulating, and transferring knowledge, as well as modifying its behavior and structure to reflect new knowledge and insights. *Self-organization is learning in practice, and synthetic technological innovation is an organizational learning process.* (Rycroft and Kash 1999, 62)

As Johnson intimates, we are on the verge or in the process of creating a new paradigm.

Many practitioners, philosophers, and researchers are profoundly interested in how this *smarter behavior* can be encouraged, how emergence and complexity are related, and how adaptation occurs in the midst of what often seems chaotic. Catalytic conversations offer a medium through which people can seek and develop smarter behavior by bringing forward their differing expertise, perspectives, values, and priorities as resources for innovation in a respectful and disciplined manner. Before looking at the nature of the environment to create enabling conditions, let us explore the role of differences among people in conversations vis-à-vis emergence.

References

Ali, S.M., and R.M. Zimmer. 1997. The question concerning emergence. http://mcs.open.ac.uk/sma78/casys97.html.

Argyris, C. 1997. *On organizational learning.* Oxford, UK: Blackwell Business.

Beeson, I., and C. Davis. 2000. Emergence and accomplishment in organizational change. *Journal of Organizational Change Management* 13 (2): 178–189.

Bennis, W. 2003. Leading edge: Dare to doubt. *CIO Insight* 1 (34): 29.

Bijlsma-Frankema, K., B. Rosendaal. and Y. Taminiau. 2006. Acting on frictions: Learning blocks and flows in knowledge intensive organizations. *Journal of European Industrial Training* 30 (4): 291–309.

Block, Peter. 2000. *Flawless consulting: A guide to getting your expertise used.* 2nd ed. San Francisco: Jossey-Bass.

Brown, J. S., and P. Duguid. 2000. *The social life of organization.* Boston: Harvard Business School Press.

Cambray, J. 2002. Synchronicity and emergence. *American Imago* 59 (4): 409–434.

Capra, F. 1982. *The turning point: Science, society, and the rising culture.* New York: Bantam Books.

———. 1991. *The tao of physics.* 3rd ed. Boston: Shambhala.

Choi, S. Y., Y. S. Kang, and H. Lee, H. 2008. The effects of socio-technical enablers on knowledge sharing: An exploratory examination. *Journal of Information Science* 34 (5): 742–754.

Dess, Gregory G., and Joseph C. Picken. 2000. Changing roles: Leadership in the 21st century. *Organizational Dynamics* 28 (3): 18–34.

Hampden-Turner, C. 1994. Foreword. In *Knowledge and value: A new perspective on corporate transformation,* ed. S. Wikstrom and R. Normann. New York: Routledge.

Hislop, D. 2002. Mission impossible? Communicating and sharing knowledge via information technology. *Journal of Information Technology* 17: 165–177.

Johnson, S. 2001. *Emergence: The connected lives of ants, brains, cities, and software.* New York: Simon and Schuster.

Joint Research Centre of the European Commission. 2000. *Futures project synthesis report.* January.

Kauffman, S., 1995. *At home in the universe: The search for the laws of self-organization and complexity.* New York: Oxford University Press.

Kim, S., and H. Lee. 2006. The impact of organizational context and information technology on employee knowledge-sharing capabilities. *Public Administration Review* 66 (3): 370–385.

Nonaka, I. 1994. A dynamic theory of organizational knowledge creation. *Organization Science* 5 (1): 14–37.

Orlikowski, W. J. 2002. Knowing in practice: Enacting a collective capability in distributed organizing. *Organization Science* 13 (3): 249–273.

Parsons, T. 1937. *The structure of social action.* New York: McGraw-Hill.

Rycroft, R. W., and D. E. Kash. 1999. *The complexity challenge: Technological innovation for the 21st century.* New York: Pinter.

Santa Fe Institute. 2009. *About SFI.* www.santafe.edu/aboutsfi/faq.php.

Sawyer, R. K. 2002. Emergence in psychology: Lessons from the history of non-reductionist science. *Human Development* 45: 2–28.

Shaw, P. 2002. *Changing conversations in organizations: A complexity approach to change.* New York: Routledge.

Stiglitz, J. E. 1999. *Public policy for a knowledge economy.* http://www.worldbank.org/html/extdr/extme/knowledge-economy.pdf.

Tymon, Walter G., and Stephen A. Stumpt. 2003. Social capital in the success of knowledge workers. *Career Development International* 8 (1): 12–20.

Waldrop, M. 1992. *Complexity: The emerging science at the edge of order and chaos.* New York: Simon and Schuster.

Wenger, E. 1998. *Communities of practice: Learning, meaning, and identity.* New York: Cambridge University Press.

4

Diverse Perspectives for Generative Change

At a deeper level, we need to realize that *understanding and misunderstanding always occur together.* . . . it is by the very process of "misunderstanding" others—that is, interpreting their claims and beliefs in slightly different terms than they do themselves—that the process of communication actually moves forward to new understanding. This is partly why we engage in conversation. (italics in original) (Burbules and Rice 1991, 17)

Differences and *misunderstandings* present problems and opportunities in organizations. Organizational stakeholders include people who represent a vast array of differences—e.g., of professional and educational background, culture, nationality, gender, religion, race, intellectual and physical ability, sexual orientation, beliefs, and values. Learning how to draw on and benefit from the understandings and misunderstandings that accompany such vast diversity is a major organizational challenge.

When people are willing to talk through misunderstandings and are competent to do so, changes occur. Participant perspectives expand as they learn from their various experiences and interpretations. Misunderstandings are akin to catalysts embedded in the conversations. They can spark catalytic conversations that help people develop *new understandings* as a foundation for generative change efforts. Participants learn through these interactions and, as a result, make more fully informed decisions and anticipate what is ahead more effectively. Their capacity for recognizing potential opportunities increases because they are pulling from a wider spectrum of information, knowledge, and experience.

Differences Are . . .

The working definition of *differences* in this book is "any attribute that people use to tell themselves another person is different" (Williams and O'Reilly 1998, 81). This definition is broad and inclusive and, most importantly, reveals that the perception of difference originates with the perceiver. At the same time, the perceiver is part of a socially constructed world that influences the perceptions.

Differences among people can be interesting, intriguing inducements for breaking down barriers when they spark new ideas, relationships, knowledge, and innovation (Argyris 1994, 1997; Baker, Jensen, and Kolb 2002; Choo 1998; Fiumara 1990; Johnson and Johnson 1989; Pearce 1995; Richter 1998; Rycroft and Kash 1999; Schrage 1990). These kinds of interactions encourage the development of inclusive and innovative working environments. Alternatively, differences can be sources of angst, avoidance, alienation, and barriers that impede constructive work. They can be a factor in the erosion of relationships and separation of people. Differences can also contribute to a sense of apathy when people feel beleaguered and unacknowledged. Whether positive or negative, differences are the grit and grindstone that in turn influence future interactions.

Tapping into Positive Behavior

What can organizations do to tap into these more positive behaviors?

> Derrida and other poststructuralists insist that the *relations* that bind and the *spaces* that distinguish cultural elements are themselves in constant interaction, so that—as [in] . . . Heisenberg's measure of motion and position for subatomic particles—each changes as one attempts to fix the other. (italics in original) (Burbules and Rice 1991, 400)

There are strong parallels between the constant interactions of sub-atomic particles and the bubbling up of differences among people in organizations. As people in *relationships* communicate across culturally distinct *spaces,* changes occur. When people *attempt to fix* one another— i.e., influence or change each other—complex dynamics affect receptivity to the differences. The quality of coworkers' relationships influences perceptions and openness. Expectations likewise shape what people see and hear and whether they think they will receive the benefit of the doubt. When people have strong trusting relationships, their receptivity to each other usually increases. The tone of the conversational *space* and the participants' competence to engage in constructive conversation also influence what they say, hear, and interpret. A conversational space in which participants make genuine efforts to communicate effectively and one in which they take time to listen and reflect usually increases receptivity. Thus, relationships, expectations, conversational spaces, and competencies all affect interpretations and the sense people make as they encounter differences.

Recognizing Relative Importance

Another factor that influences sense making is that the things one person or group considers to be important are not necessarily of equal importance to another. If a difference does not matter to a person, he or she may not even notice it. For instance, punctuality is more critical to some than to others. When you are on the way to an appointment and you encounter a friend or colleague who stops to talk, what is your typical inclination? For some people punctuality is primary, while for others being exactly on time for the appointment matters less than taking the time to talk to the friend or colleague. Thus, for this latter group, being late is more acceptable than rushing away from an incomplete conversation. These differing interpretations of what is appropriate, polite, and respectful behavior are usually deeply rooted in cultural patterns and learned early in life. In other words, they are unexamined, and thus unconscious, assumptions operating among people who do not even realize that others with the best intentions have differing priorities. The differences function like mirror images that churn up considerable organizational misunderstanding, angst, and stress.

If Mark does not particularly value punctuality, he is unlikely to try to *fix* or change another person's tardiness. On the other hand, if Tom and Mark work together and Tom perceives punctuality as critical to productivity, which he values, and an indicator of respect for the person who is kept waiting, he may want to *fix* Mark to get him to be more punctual. "Differences that may not be apparent to, or salient for, others may be paramount in the minds of the individuals at hand . . . 'difference' (or its absence) cannot always be inferred or assumed from the outside" (Burbules and Rice 1991, 15). Herein is an important point that reaffirms the definition of *differences* cited earlier. The perceptions of the differences originate within the perceiver. People can fuel misunderstandings and seriously damage valued relationships when they try to interpret right from wrong *for other* people without asking questions and trying to understand the sources of differences.

When differences are more important to one person or group than another, ignoring them rarely works. If Tom and Mark try to ignore their differing perceptions about punctuality, the problem festers and grows over time. An alternative that may seem simplistic is to talk through the misunderstandings. Taking the initiative and time to have the conversation, asking questions and listening carefully to each other to explore the misunderstandings, and considering future adjustments may avoid a lot of angst, while strengthening trusting relationships at the same time.

Conversations are a seriously undervalued and untapped resource for coping with differences in complex, changing environments. Rather than *inferring* or *assuming* the intentions of others, conversations are a medium for asking questions, hearing new information, trying to understand, and learning from colleagues. In constructive conversations, participants delve below the surface to explore reasons, thoughts, feelings, and intentions, making it possible to express themselves and to respond to each other.

To return to our example, as they talk through their conflict, Tom recognizes that Mark highly values each person with whom he talks and does not want to be rude by ending a conversation abruptly. On reflection, Tom realizes that Mark gives him that kind of attention when they are talking. Mark recognizes that Tom has a tight schedule of back-to-back appointments and that Tom depends on him. They realize anew their mutual respect for each other and that neither one intends to be rude or thoughtless. As they iteratively adapt, create, and recreate interpretations and organizational norms, they gain insight into their unconscious assumptions and differing perspectives as they plan ways to work more effectively in the future. Thus, they have a catalytic conversation and generate positive plans while also strengthening their relationship.

Microlevel and Macrolevel Interdependence

What does conversation have to do with the macrolevel mission and purpose of an organization? What is the connection between macrolevel organizational dynamics and the interpersonal interactions among people? Interestingly, these two issues are inextricably interdependent.

Historically, traditional models of leadership were almost exclusively hierarchical and authoritarian in most religious, sovereign, and other governing institutions. It is therefore not surprising that when organizations first began to proliferate in the early twentieth century, they replicated the familiar models of leadership—i.e., organizational structures with top-down, hierarchical, command-and-control decision-making structures.

However, during the last few decades of the twentieth century and the beginning of the twenty-first century, organizational success increasingly required different kinds of leadership and more entrepreneurial, team-based, flexible, and open approaches associated with innovation. Furthermore, younger workers in Western nations expect to have more input and influence at work than their grandparents did. Multidirectional communication patterns in organizations are much more common. Communication is not only top-down. To become or remain competitive, organizations must be able to attract and retain the most talented young workers as baby boomers retire. This change is a good illustration of the interface of macrolevel shifts in changing economies and microlevel expectations about appropriate ways of leading and organizing people.

Although the role of macrolevel influences is widely accepted in Western literature, the role of microlevel conversations on macro structures is less well developed. In contrast, Engestrom and Middleton's book (1996) of in-depth case studies demonstrates how organizational contexts and structures emerge out of the local, daily interactions and behaviors among people. Engestrom and Middleton say that, " . . . contexts and structures of work are regarded as outcomes of local interactions and negotiations" (p. 2). In other words, the interpersonal dynamics (at the micro level) give shape to organizational structures and contexts (at the macro level). Simultaneously, the macrolevel patterns are also influencing the microlevel webs of complex interactions and interdependencies.

Microlevel conversations influence and give shape to the organizational culture as the macrolevel policies perpetuate certain norms and thus, in turn, shape future interpersonal conversations and behaviors. Trying to understand the complexity of organizational life without incorporating these mutually interdependent processes is like looking at either the individual behaviors of people who make their living by fishing or international trade policy to try to understand fluctuating fisheries ecology. Either approach in isolation will give skewed results.

To understand the dynamics of a particular environment, it is essential

to observe and focus on patterns at the broad, macro level of organizations and the larger society as well as at the interpersonal communication
patterns among stakeholders. For example, consider the dynamics of
a large change effort in an organization that has a strong, competitive
win/lose culture. At the interpersonal level, individuals fear losing influence or being perceived as losing influence in the change effort, thus
increasing resistance to change. The pressure *for* change and resistance
to change build up even more intensely. Those dynamics buck up against
the macrolevel pressure for the change, creating high-tension stalemates.
Without addressing the organizational culture and goals in conjunction
with the microlevel norms about how people work together, long-term
systemic change is doomed. There need to be simultaneous cultural
shifts at the micro and macro level away from a win/lose context—i.e.,
a form of either/or behavior—to unlock the potential for new kinds of
interaction. Policy changes can be made to discourage win/lose behavior such as rewards and incentives for teamwork and requirements for
broader participation in early planning processes. It is similarly possible
to identify ways to make changes at the micro level that reinforce, rather
than undermine, each other, such as building acceptance and competency
for conversational learning and catalytic conversations.

Looking Back and Seeing Ahead

Generative change processes serve as a tether between the past and
the future. Because generative change is intentional, expansive, and
collaborative, the people involved listen carefully, especially to their
differences, and talk through misunderstandings as they try to learn
together and better understand each other. This relational, contextual
learning provides participants with the knowledge they need to shape
their future according to shared goals, ideals, and visions. In essence,
they "are continuously constructing the future together as the movement
of sense making in the present" (Shaw 2003, 129).

At the same time, when participants have the competencies for these
kinds of conversations, as they grapple with issues, they do not give
up who they are. They bring their individual and collective origins and
priorities into the conversation, are able to consider differing perspectives, and can incorporate new aspects of them. As they bring their own
values, wisdom, and knowledge into the conversation and hear others,
they may take some of what they learn and incorporate it into their own

perspective. If not, they may at least understand the differing perspectives more fully. In the words of David Mathews (1995), who has been deeply involved in civil discourse, people "may not change their own opinions about an issue, but they are quite likely to change their opinions of other people's opinions" (p. 28).

Thus, as people make changes in light of what came before and what they hope for the future, they do not bounce from one fad to another, nor do they resist change altogether. They do not change for the sake of change or for the sake of taking action. By looking back and seeing ahead they *intentionally incorporate the past that they want to bring forward into the future that they want to create.*

Thomas and Ely (1996) describe a decidedly relevant perspective emerging in organizational life—what they call the "learning-and-effectiveness" paradigm. This "new model for managing diversity lets the organization internalize differences among employees so that it learns and grows because of them" (p. 86). *Internalizing,* as distinct from avoiding or only *talking about* the differences, provokes systemic and generative change. This internalization process is similar to what Nonaka (1994) describes as a critical element of knowledge creation and organizational learning. Organizations benefit by learning from their diverse employees and integrating the new learning by using it, by making changes in business practices, revising an organizational mission, or rethinking marketing strategies, for example. This process is profoundly different from simply gathering information or addressing immediate symptomatic problems in that it is continuous and ongoing. In other words, under this new paradigm, as new and diverse voices enter and have influence, the norms do not become reified. Instead, the people involved are continually learning with diverse others and mutually adapting in constructive ways.

Thomas and Ely use the example of a successful, small, public interest, all-white law firm that was one of their field research sites. As people in the firm realized how often their employment-related cases involved nonwhite clients, they hired a Latina woman. They expected that she would be an asset for these cases and would help bring in more clients that were ethnically and racially diverse. However, the firm gained far more than it expected and became a model of the learning-and-effectiveness paradigm. "The new attorney introduced ideas . . . about what kinds of cases [the firm] should take on . . . More women of color were hired . . . [and] they now pursue cases that its previously all-white legal staff would not have thought relevant . . . because the link between the firm's mission and the employment issues involved in the cases would not have been obvious to them" (Thomas and Ely 1996, 85).

In other words, as the new and original members of the firm worked and talked together over time, they gradually internalized differing perspectives and learned enough from each other to see and respond to unexpected possibilities. This public interest law firm did not abandon its original mission or compromise its integrity. Instead, the firm expanded its thinking to see opportunities that it had never before imagined, extending its mission into new areas of public interest law. As the new nonwhite lawyers in the firm learned about the mission and work of the law firm, they were subsequently able to recognize and articulate wider opportunities for collaboration. As the former and new attorneys worked together effectively to learn from and internalize their differences, they engaged in generative change processes.

Thomas and Ely (1996) offer other examples of organizations operating within this new learning-and-effectiveness paradigm. Traditionally, as new people entered organizations they faced unmistakable pressure to conform; the dominant norms prevailed. These more traditional organizations expected complete assimilation, instead of assuming that new *and* former employees could all engage in some degree of change. When newcomers are expected to do all of the conforming and assimilating, they frequently suppress much of their energy, expertise, and experience. When full one-sided assimilation is the prevailing assumption, the organization unknowingly loses much of the new talent of its new hires, who could revitalize the organization in creative and productive ways.

Within the learning-and-effectiveness perspective, however, the responsibility for change shifts. It is no longer the sole responsibility of newcomers to change. This fundamental shift means that organizational stakeholders confront their differences in ongoing learning conversations and catalytic conversations that promote webs of mutual learning, that is, to develop the tether between the past and the future. Employees throughout the organization share responsibility to learn from each other. The organization expects to be surprised by and to learn from newcomers.

The organization must also recognize its long-term employees as treasure troves of organizational knowledge and continuity. These more innovative organizations are less likely to push such employees out the door, let them go easily, or encourage them to retire early. Instead, they try to find ways for employees who embody organizational history and knowledge to continue to contribute in a variety of part- or full-time capacities. The newcomer and the "old hand" are both included in the web of mutual learning.

The learning-and-effectiveness approach (Thomas and Ely 1996) is especially relevant to this book. Complex economies demand vastly diverse and interdependent expertise, experiences, talents, and perspectives. As described in the previous chapter, Thomas and Ely's work demonstrates fundamentally new approaches emerging in contemporary organizations that resemble a paradigm shift. This paradigm,

> . . . organizes itself around the overarching theme of integration. Assimilation goes too far in pursuing sameness. Differentiation . . . overshoots in the other direction. . . . [T]his new model . . . lets the organization internalize differences among employees so that it learns and grows because of them. (Thomas and Ely 1996, 86)

Internalization and integration are elements of generative change that strengthen the tether between the past and the future. Have no illusion that diverse people are easily integrated or that indiscriminate integration is beneficial. By incorporating a shift toward the learning-and-effectiveness approach, organizations can take better advantage of the concrete benefits that diversity brings to most kinds of work (Baker et al. 2002; Brown and Duguid 1991, 2000; Eisenhardt, Kahwajy, and Bourgeois 1997; Nonaka 1994; Nonaka and Takeuchi 1995; Tjosvold, and Sun 2002; Tjosvold, Law, and Sun 2003). Thus, generative changes within organizations and with external environments require a rethinking of deeply embedded traditional cultural assumptions about assimilation.

Institutionalization of Culture

Cultural patterns and norms evolve slowly. One generation passes its values, beliefs, procedures, rituals, and customs to the next generation by institutionalizing its cultural norms. For example, educational systems and parenting practices, organizational hiring practices, and training programs are all cultural institutions that instill expectations and norms in children and new employees from one societal or organizational generation to the next. Judicial systems and grievance procedures, media, and marketing represent additional examples of the institutionalization of culture.

The cultural institutions of any organization or society are the mediums for that organization or society's preservation, for these institutions frame and reinforce what is expected and acceptable. Who is educated and trained, what they are taught and not taught, and whether ongoing learning is important are all markers of the priorities of a culture. As institutions shape people's preparation for work and life and mold the minds, expectations, and worldviews of one generation after another, norms emerge regarding many values, such as conformity and nonconformity.

Cultural institutions change slowly and even more so where the pressure to conform is heavy and homogeneity prevails. Because change in the global economies and diverse populations in the twenty-first century is a pervasive given, organizations that can accept nonconformity are more likely to be viable. Moreover, being able to thrive in the transition zone at the edge of chaos depends upon enough nonconformity for flexibility, surprise, and the capacity for disagreement. Organizational cultures that are not open to differences threaten the health, and even the viability, of the organization.

To become more aware of specific cultural institutions in your world, think about what is encouraged and discouraged in the culture of your organization or your family, your community, or country. Notice the institutional practices that shape the communication patterns, training and development programs, and planning and budgetary practices that sustain the culture in your organizations. Cultural norms and institutions determine who has influence, who has opportunity for further education and training, who has access to information, who participates in decision making, and who controls resource distribution. Are these institutional practices serving your organization, family, community, or country well in a changing world?

Contrasting Worldviews

Another way to gain understanding into organizational culture is to explore stakeholders' worldviews. There are many theoretical models used to describe contrasting macrolevel cultural patterns (Hampden-Turner and Trompenaars 1993, 2000; Hofstede 1991; Lewis 1999). Generally, these models are presented as broad dialectical extremes—e.g., the communitarian-individualistic distinction. These dialectics are dangerously misleading if used as categories to group or label people. They can however help to identify broad contrasts to expand thinking into unfamiliar worldviews. By learning about the patterns of behavior and priorities at dialectical extremes and the range of differences between the extremes, unconscious assumptions get exposure. The purpose is to open new possibilities, not to encourage adversarial patterns of *either/or* thinking. It is not to dismiss one extreme or to assert the other. Instead, the challenge is to find common ground and build mutual respect for differing worldviews.

To demonstrate, let's look at the juxtaposition of cultures in a communitarian-individualistic dialectic. At one extreme, people with strong communitarian values emphasize harmony and the interests of the group or community as a whole, as distinct from the other extreme where the well-being of the individual is a stronger cultural norm (Hampden-Turner and Trompenaars 1993, 2000; Hofstede 1991). Theoretically, either the community or the individual is valued at the extremes. But people rarely function at either extreme and instead generally value both points of view, although to differing degrees. To weigh your priorities, ask yourself questions such as, "Should we pay heed to individual convictions and dissenting ideas . . . or should the welfare of the wider group, corporation, and society, consisting as these do of multiple persons, be our principal concern?" (Hampden-Turner and Trompenaars 2000, 68–69).

In a more communitarian culture, maintaining harmony and working with others toward the success of the group as a whole take priority over individual convictions or achievements. The tendency is to shun individuals who stand out from the crowd because of their personal success, expertise, or beliefs because individual well-being at the expense of group harmony is inappropriate and considered arrogant. Conversely, in an individualistic environment, the well-being, ideas, and achievements of the individual are considered to be relatively more important than attending to the team or communitarian unit as a whole.

To gain insight into the prevailing worldviews in your own organization, think once again about the behaviors that are encouraged, rewarded, and used for performance reviews, evaluations, and promotions, for example. Is contribution to the team or organization as a whole valued more or less than individual work? In the United States, it is common for an organization to verbally encourage teamwork and yet base an employee's performance evaluations, promotions, and salary increases solely on individual achievement. Verbally encouraging teamwork while basing incentives and rewards on individual achievement creates incongruity that is confusing and inconsistent. This discrepancy is an example of the difference between an organization's proclaimed principles (talk) and actual behavior (walk); that is, the organization that is not *walking its own talk* (Argyris 1994, 1997).

Universality and Particularism

Another dialectical continuum, *universalism* and *particularism,* is used by many researchers to describe opposite extremes of cultural patterns (Hampden-Turner and Trompenaars 1993, 2000; Hofstede 1991). According to Hampden-Turner and Trompenaars (2000), some cultures strive to establish common, universal sets of standards, laws, and rules that apply consistently to everyone. An extreme example is a rigid bureaucracy in which people follow formal policies and procedures, regardless of the situation or the impact on individuals in unusual circumstances. Because, theoretically, there is a rule or universal standard for whatever occurs, people working in rigidly bureaucratic organizations do not have the authority to consider individual differences. Less extreme universalistic organizations have standards and criteria for hiring or promotion to discourage favoritism while also accommodating unusual circumstances. These less rigid universal standards give people relatively clear, upfront evaluation criteria while allowing varying degrees of discretion.

In a particularistic culture, consideration for specific situations takes precedence over universal standards. A strong example is the common hiring practice of giving priority to candidates who are in similar social networks rather than to strangers with specific expertise and experience. These patterns may also relate to cultural norms about trust (Fukuyama 1995). When a culture's norm regarding trust of others in business, for example, does not extend beyond family members, the specific expertise of a stranger has less primacy. In a more moderate situation, there is a preference to hire employees who are at least part of a broad social network, along with consideration for the expertise and experience needed for specific jobs.

Through the lens of universalism, the focus is on the commonality among people. Driven by the importance of fairness and justice to all, at least theoretically, laws and rules should apply equally to everyone (Hampden-Turner and Trompenaars 2000). The foundation of the U.S. judicial system rests on this standard of equal treatment. The U.S.

Figure 4.1 **Dialectic of universalism and particularism**

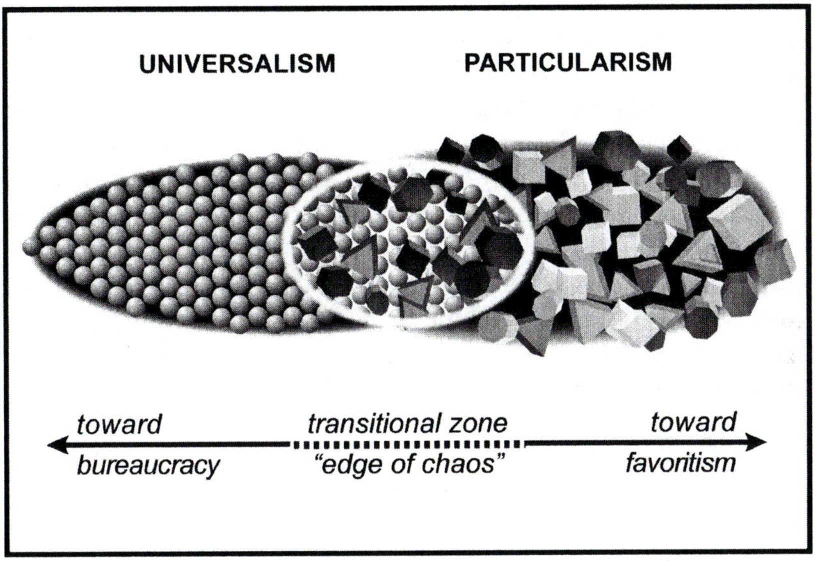

governmental, legal, and often organizational propensity is toward universalism.

An alternate way of framing the world is as a mirror image (Hampden-Turner and Trompenaars 2000). From the perspective of particularism, protecting relationships and differing circumstances requires in-depth consideration of relationships and specific situations. At the extreme, promotions and rewards go to family members or good friends, for example, even when an individual is not qualified. The value of the relationship takes priority over specific qualifications or performance. Yet working in diverse settings and working at the edge of chaos require a blend of the two extremes (Figure 4.1).

Let's explore an example of an organization with a strictly universal policy that all employees must be physically present in the workplace during regular working hours. Suppose a conscientious employee's spouse is diagnosed with cancer and needs extensive chemotherapy. In a strong universalistic culture where all policies should apply evenly, management is likely to feel reluctant to make exceptions. In a more particularistic culture, the cultural norms give the manager considerable discretion to negotiate a flexible agreement with the employee regarding work hours and work site.

When juxtaposing the extreme universal versus the particular, one way to articulate the difference is to ask, "[s]hould we apply . . . the most appropriate rule, even if the fit is inexact, or do special circumstances and unique occurrences raise questions about the rule itself? (Hampden-Turner and Trompenaars 2000, 13). The worldview of managers usually influences how strictly they adhere to these norms when exceptional circumstances occur. It may be difficult for the manager with strong allegiance to universal treatment regardless of circumstances to allow employees much flexibility. On the other hand, the person whose world-view is more particularistic may find it easier to be flexible and more challenging to impose a universal standard.

Differences in Power

Decision-making patterns such as those just discussed raise critical questions about the use of power and how differences among people affect who has influence and how it is used. In organizations, there are always people and groups who have more power than others. Power inequities, whether of opinion and values or of race and nationality, are embedded in most relationships. There can be blatant, concrete, specific power inequities, such as a boss who uses hierarchical power indiscriminately to dominate employees. Differences in power can also be quite subtle.

Power inequities influence the conversational patterns that groups develop. The patterns are usually unconscious and thus especially difficult to change (Case 1992; Gersick 1988). For example, one person in a meeting makes a suggestion and everyone ignores it. Later in the same meeting, another person makes the same suggestion, and this time participants take it seriously and endorse the idea. Although the possible reasons for the differing responses are varied, considerable research on similar situations confirms that people considered part of the dominant group are more likely to be listened to than are members of nondominant groups (Barrett 2004; Krolokke and Sorensen 2006). Over time, these patterns are insidious as they undermine or block the input of divergent perspectives and become ingrained as appropriate "business-as-usual" norms. The greatest danger is when participants do not recognize their own patterns and thus do not see how they limit adaptability and smother innovation. Therefore, groups and subsequently organizations limit their access to the points of view of a subgroup of leaders, which may also be the least likely sources of divergent, innovative ideas.

When group members become astute observers of group processes and conversational patterns, they begin to recognize and can change norms that do not serve the group or organization. When they are more aware of these subtle sources of power as they are played out through conversations, participants are better able to access and use their personal power constructively. As they develop more skill with these kinds of conversations, they become somewhat less vulnerable to manipulation and abuse. Thus, it is imperative to notice which participants speak and who is heard, discouraged, ignored, or unacknowledged. Even without explicit criticism or exclusion, people who are chronically unacknowledged typically leave the organization when they have a chance or they become apathetic and sometimes counter-productive. The result is a drain of talent and high turnover costs.

Subtle, conversational patterns that silence diverse perspectives perpetuate the status quo by limiting alternative points of view. Unrecognized conversational patterns that reinforce arbitrary power imbalances damage organizations. Ignoring the patterns perpetuates them. By seeing them and evaluating each one in light of context and impact, the range of choices widens. Participants can then intentionally try to change the patterns.

Universality and the Politics of Difference

In this section, I deliberately change the term *particularism* to the *politics of difference* to highlight a specific meaning related to the previous section. Differences are not all equal. From the perspective of the politics of difference, some inequities are so important that they demand special consideration. Differences that violate and institutionalize gross power imbalances and disparities of fundamental rights and opportunities are the politics of difference and need to be changed. The premise of this perspective is that organizations and societies are responsible for the impact of their policies, laws, and rules and thus in some cases have a responsibility to rethink or moderate universal laws and standards.

The most negative effects of power inequities typically grow out of implicit, unexamined assumptions that "difference means deficiency"; that is, the " . . . fear of difference springs from the dominant-subordinate tradition in which difference means deficiency" (Miller 1986, 137). The politics of difference perspective calls for heightened awareness and responsibility for assumptions that differences imply deficiency. Let's explore the possible implications.

Organizations socialize new people into the prevailing norms, which include prevailing biases. Likewise, as children grow up and parents and other family members pass on their values, they also pass on biases. For example, if I want to encourage my children to recognize the importance of school and performance I might encourage them to find friends who also do well. Thus, even if only implicitly, I may send a message to my children that negatively identifies and isolates a group of people (i.e., children whom I think make bad grades in school).

To communicate my values, I may use broad generalizations about children who do well in school. In the process, even though unintended, I pass on at least two major biases. One is the assumption that my children and I will be able to identify accurately the students who are performing well when it is difficult enough for good teachers to make those assessments. Another implicit assumption is that a child who makes good grades is superior. By broadly highlighting one group as superior, I implicitly communicate that the contrasting group is inferior. Thus, even with the best intentions, I pass on an insidious message that difference means less than.

Differences perceived as deficiencies are gross generalizations, although easily absorbed messages, from the surrounding environment. Negative generalizations about groups of people undermine the potential for peerlike, collaborative relationships among people who are *different*. Research and work on the politics of difference offer provocative, important insight into these dynamics (Crawford 1989; Henley and Kramarae 1991; Kersten 2000).

Universal standards imply broad commonality among people in an organization. Where all else is equal, universal standards are fair and make sense. But not all people are equal and neither are all differences. The institutionalized exclusion of people because of stereotyping based on categories such as race, gender, sexual orientation, and age reinforces power inequities and unfairly perpetuates the status quo and arbitrary exclusion. The more rigidly people insist on justice as a universal standard, without inquiry into other possibilities, the harder it may be to see the power dynamics. Assuming all differences are of equal importance relieves people in dominant groups of the responsibility for change because they are not accountable for the negative impact of power inequities (Crawford 1989; Kersten 2000).

For example, the following statement is often heard in the United States and perhaps other parts of the world:

If those people would just work hard, they could be successful too.

The underlying assumption in this statement is that the only variable among people is how hard they work. The implicit assumption is that everyone has the same access to good education, good health, well-paying jobs, and other entrees to success. Everyone who works hard can be successful. The statement reflects an extreme universalistic perspective that differences among people are equally important and equally malleable to change.

Universalism and the politics of difference each represent distinct worldviews that in turn influence perceptions of differences. The worldviews affect individual and organizational priorities and decision making (i.e., their sense making). Once again, a dialectical tension between two extreme perspectives comes into view. Are there differences that should temper universal laws and standards? And if so, which ones? When and how much? These questions are only examples of the possibilities. While individuals grapple with them to form their values and priorities, so do organizations and cultures. I am suggesting that suppressing the tension or accepting norms that discourage this grappling make change unlikely. It is in the process of engaging such questions and the ongoing reevaluation of norms that adaptation and innovation can thrive. In essence, people must be able to engage substantially about these differences and therefore to engage at the edge of chaos as needed for ongoing learning and new knowledge creation.

To revisit the contrasting perspectives, from a universalistic vantage point, people tend to strive for unity and tranquility by addressing all differences with a unified set of laws, standards, and rules. Justice, fairness, and stability require that all people and groups be treated the same according to a unified standard.

From a politics of difference perspective, universalism makes it difficult to increase access to less powerful individuals and groups. It perpetuates the status quo. These institutionalized norms function as not-so-silent expectations in organizations. Because historically some groups had less access and power, the status quo denies them fundamental rights. Because world events engender fear, universal standards limit the rights of whole groups, such as the Japanese Americans in the United States during World War II. These patterns impede change. According to a politics of difference worldview, the high priority for unity and tranquility (i.e., maintaining the status quo) encourages assimilation and groupthink to the detriment of change and innovation.

In summary, when the desire for unity and calm supersedes the need to reevaluate institutionalized norms, or universalism, the pressure to change is alleviated. When the urgency to reevaluate norms because of injustice supersedes the desire for unity the pressure for change intensifies. I suggest that resolution of the tension between worldviews is never complete as revisiting the issues and difficult questions are at the core of integrity. At the same time, quality of life and accomplishment of work require more than brief respites from the intense tension and work at the edge of chaos. Yet when the exploration of differences is a part of everyday interaction, the intensity of the confrontation is dramatically reduced. Questions come up earlier, and participants make smaller, more frequent, adjustments.

Assumptions about Rational Problem Solving

A commitment to universalism rests on the assumption that people construct policies, standards, and laws rationally and objectively. In practice, however, there are limits to the rationality and objectivity of human beings. Cultural norms and human behavior emerge out of countless complex pressures, fears, and desires. Often people behave in ways that are not in their own best interest or in the organization's best interest due to a fear of losing a job, saving face, overly zealous ambition, excessive stress, illness, and so on. As described in the previous chapter, the volatility at the edge of chaos is a more accurate description of organizational dynamics than the rationality of linear cause-and-effect thinking. In addition, because of a lack of direct life experience and a lack of direct honest communication, people in dominant groups are less likely to be aware of the experiences, issues, and the needs of people who are different, that is, who are the *others*. In general, universal standards have not accounted for these differences.

Fifty years ago flextime, which allows employees the flexibility to stagger the hours and days of their work schedules, was extremely rare in U.S. organizations. The standards were established by decision makers who were typically people in homogeneous dominant groups, and those standards reflected their lifestyle, work patterns, and inherited assumptions about organizational norms. The assumption in part was that consistent, uniform work schedules (i.e., a universal standard) represented the best way to do business and to be fair to everyone. However, demography drove change in the workplace as a diversity of populations led to a less homogeneous workforce. In the 1960s, the civil rights movement gradually brought far more people of color into a wider range of jobs, and the feminist movement and changing economic pressures brought more women into the workplace.

Pressure for change increased. The demography of employees and organizational leaders changed substantially, bringing the previous universal standards under unprecedented scrutiny. The workforce now includes far more women and a far greater proportion of workers who come from homes with two working adults without a stay-at-home adult. Thus, the decision makers formulating standards in most organizations are more diverse and reflect a wider range of experiences. Organizational standards regarding face time (in person) and non–face time (remote or off-hour) at work are not uniform. Flextime became much more common, even when telecommuting is not a factor and before it was an option.

Fifty years ago, however, there were also many workers supporting families without a stay-at-home adult. They also needed flextime. Nevertheless, these workers were rarely part of the dominant groups who were setting the standards, thus limiting their influence to change those standards. It was not until the demography changed and the dominant groups became more diverse that the push for change succeeded. Although there are additional factors, this compelling example illustrates how a lack of direct experience contributes to perpetuation of the status quo, which in this case was a universal standard. The example also demonstrates how important it is for people affected by rules, procedures, or standards to have substantive input in decision making. When people affected by changes are a part of the conversation and are able to offer their perspectives, they are more likely to resonate with the resulting changes (Baker et al. 2002; Habermas 1991). The quality of decisions is improved by gaining wider input. Thus, organizations need to bring people who are more diverse into the conversations and decision making of the workplace.

A prerequisite to systemic change is recognition and consideration of unexamined assumptions. Potent embedded assumptions influence perception of terms such as *deficiency* and *less than* (Crawford 1989; Henley and Kramarae 1991; Kersten 2000). Gathering diverse input and acknowledging power inequities embedded in archetypal images such as *deficiency* and *less than* make it easier to be more aware of unconscious norms. It is a first step on an earnest journey to discover how to communicate, work, and organize more effectively. (This topic is developed in Part II.) It is important to explore the role of privilege vis-à-vis differences in organizations.

The Privilege of Not Being Different

Generally, the definition of *privilege* is an advantage, immunity, or right granted to a particular person or group. Primarily the use of the word *privilege* in this context distinguishes between people who are a part of a dominant group and those perceived by the dominants as different or *other.* The word *privilege* is not used here as an indicator of financial wealth or a caste system. Many people who are a part of a dominant group do not have that kind of privilege, at least not in the United States.

The focus here is on social groups who have always had a privilege—such as males or tall people—because it is difficult to recognize a privilege when it is so much a part of a person's life experience. It is similar to the air that humans breathe and the water in which fish swim. Until there is a threat to the supply or quality of air or water, it is difficult to be aware of it without any experience of living without it. It is easy to take it for granted.

To illustrate the meaning of privilege and the interface of the micro and macro dynamics, consider the authors of the U.S. Constitution. In 1789 this group created a government to protect the rights and equality of all. Many people revere the Constitution as a hallmark of democratic governance. Yet, ironically, all human behavior grows out of experience, and in some ways the authors of the U.S. Constitution were no different.

In a democracy, the most fundamental right and form of participation is the right to vote, and these authors granted people the right to vote. Yet the vote was limited to people like themselves—white, male property owners. Men of color could not vote in the United States until the adoption of the Fifteenth Amendment in 1870, and women could not vote until 1920 with the adoption of the Nineteenth Amendment. In fact, landless white men could not vote until 1856. Giving people the right to vote was a notable milestone, but the limitations of who could vote reflect the limits of the authors' experience, or their *privilege.*

My intention is not to diminish the importance and achievement of the authors or the Constitution. However, it is to illustrate how difficult it is to see outside of one's own experiences because the filters of experience limit perspective without intentional, concentrated efforts to understand beyond one's personal experience. Part of intentionality involves exposure to, conversation with, and experience with diverse others. It also requires working outside of underlying assumptions about differences as deficiencies.

As with most privilege, it is possible to provide logical reasons to support the status quo behavior. Yet justifications usually also reflect worldviews, priorities, and rationalizations. Throughout the nineteenth century, one of the major reasons given for prohibiting women from voting was to protect them from stresses and demands of public life that women could not handle because of their weak constitution. Today this argument is a rationalization that is hard for most people to believe. Yet it supported a prevailing point of view among people who had never lived in a democracy where all citizens had the right to vote.

Privileges function like assumed, unconscious parts of life. They are aspects of the worldview or lens through which individuals see the world, making it almost impossible to see outside of their experience without deliberate intentionality. It is easier to see one's own privilege when it is compared to others' lack of the same privilege. For example, a person who takes for granted the privilege of the physical ability to walk and move easily experiences a sharp contrast the first time he or she breaks or loses a leg or spends concentrated time with a family member or a friend in a wheelchair. Suddenly, the importance of whether there are curb slopes and elevators or room to sit in the wheelchair in a restaurant increases. The contrast becomes more visible through exposure to and experience with the *other.* By interacting in ongoing conversations and by being in relationship with the other, it is gradually easier to see the filter itself.

In the flextime example, when most managers had a stay-at-home spouse to take care of family needs, they shared a common experience. Unconscious expectations come with the privilege of spouses who did not need to work for financial reasons and whose socialization encouraged them not to work "outside of the home." As demographics changed, people without this privilege gradually changed the standards. Increasingly, not only workers but also managers who did not have the privilege of a stay-at-home adult experienced the critical need for flextime.

Metaphorically speaking, Marilyn Frye offers an image of a birdcage to illustrate how privilege works. She says that no matter how long or closely a person focuses on a single wire of a birdcage, it is hard to understand why the bird is unable to fly around, under, or over the wire to have freedom of movement. It is,

> . . . only when you step back, stop looking at the wires one by one . . . and take a macroscopic view of the whole cage that you can see why the bird does not go anywhere . . . no one [of the wires] would be the least hindrance to its flight, but which, by their relations to each other, are as confining as the solid walls of a dungeon. (Frye 2001, 50–51)

For people without privilege, the network of overlapping wires constrains their movement within the institutions of an organization, society, or global economy. A person who has a privilege, lacks experience of existing without it, and has little or no exposure and conversation with the *other* is metaphorically focusing on one wire at a time. This individual is unable to see Frye's birdcage and the large web of limitations that the cage represents. The institutionalization of privilege is like locking the door of the birdcage, making it difficult to access the larger world of the organization, society, or economy.

To demonstrate this contrast, the experience of Peggy McIntosh (2007) is illustrative. As a member of the faculty of a postsecondary women's studies program, McIntosh focused her work primarily on gender differences. She was astutely aware of privileges that she did not have as a woman. As she understood more from her lack of many of the privileges afforded to males, she gradually began for the first time to recognize the privileges that she had as a white person.

Subsequently, McIntosh wrote a classic paper in which she created a metaphor of a knapsack to illustrate the silent advantages that privilege offers. She portrayed privilege as "an invisible weightless knapsack of special provisions, assurances, tools, maps, guides, codebooks, passports, visas, clothes, compass, emergency gear, and blank checks" (McIntosh 2007). When people have the knapsack, the likelihood of having a successful and satisfying trip is better. When people do not have these kinds of provisions or privileges they are not as well prepared for a successful journey through life. It is harder to find the way, to gain access, or to find the help needed in strategic places. It is a demonstration of the uneven playing field in a world of privilege.

When a person has always had a privilege (such as being white or physically healthy or male or from the United States) and is unreflective of unconscious, cultural assumptions that accompany the privilege, it is invisible. Awareness outside of one's own experience is usually cloudy at best. To increase awareness, individuals must deliberately step outside of their own experience to see and hear more about the experiences of the other. Engaging in ongoing substantial conversation with diverse others is a critical component of stepping outside of one's own experience. Working as interdependent peers and developing relationships deepen understanding. The crux of the work and relationship is conversation.

Implications of Worldview and Privilege

Part of the invisible knapsack of privilege is that rules, laws, standards, and norms reflect the people who create them. Especially in cultures such as the United States where universality is the norm, it can be difficult to see the injustices built into the standards and laws assumed and intended to protect fairness and justice. The characteristics of the majority, the dominant groups, generally become the "not-so-subtle standards for normality, beauty, properness, professionalism and everything else" (Essed in Kersten 2000, 239). People who are hiring employees, consciously or unconsciously, set the standards for more than job requirements. Likewise, professionals set the standards for more than just the required knowledge and skill sets for their professions.

Certain types of dress, language, and jokes, for example, are appropriate in a given context while others are highly inappropriate. When people have not had access to the invisible knapsack's contents to guide them to know more about these norms, it is harder for them to learn. They may not even realize that dressing a particular way or using certain colloquialisms is inappropriate and out of place when they interview for a job in an accountant's firm or a doctor's office. There are spoken and unspoken standards about appropriate behavior, manners, dress, and presentation of self in any context. They come along with the privilege of belonging.

Not only do people already in the positions create the standards, but they also have mirror-image expectations for those in nondominant groups. When someone from a nondominant group, such as a person of color or a woman, is bold and assertive in their conversations, for example, the behavior may be perceived as inappropriate. Yet the same behavior may be desirable, even necessary, for a person in the dominant group.

People rarely talk openly in organizations about these unconscious norms and underlying expectations and so reevaluations do not occur easily. At the same time, the unspoken standards are typically a vital part of the evaluation of others. These expectations and norms function as an almost impossible barrier to people who lack the knapsack of provisions. These barriers do not serve the organizations that create them, because they make it more difficult for the organizations to bring in the diverse people they need to reflect their diverse stakeholders and to stimulate new ideas, change, and innovation.

Unless diverse people are included in formal and informal conversations and decision making, the catalysts to rethink expectations and reconsider taken-for-granted assumptions are usually missing. In addition, it is not enough for people with diverse perspectives to be physically present. They must also be active, acknowledged voices in the conversations and decision making, meaning that the organizational culture has to adapt. Conversations that effectively challenge long-held expectations and assumptions require conversational competence and enabling conversational contexts (Nonaka 1994). People have to learn constructive ways to disagree. Part II of this book addresses the infrastructure considerations needed for more effective organizational conversation through conversational learning and catalytic conversations.

Without ongoing exploration of differences and active inclusion of diverse perspectives, vast resources remained untapped. Anger and resentment build. Potentially, the organization sows the seeds for its own demise. People from traditionally dominant and nondominant groups all share responsibility for fostering full participation.

Conclusions

Often, differences make it especially difficult to stay in the transitional space at the edge of chaos long enough to reap the benefits. If differences seem too threatening, people may be inclined to retreat into a more orderly, comfortable, and seemingly more predictable environment. Alternatively, if people do not modulate their differences, organizations can slip into a state of chaos. It is in learning more about how to work with differences that people can become more adept at juggling them constructively.

I suggest that part of the perception of differences originates within each person, thus honoring the legitimacy of alternative perspectives. At the same time, because people enact at least part of the perception of differences socially, the weight of responsibility is on each person and each organization to be involved in ongoing intentional conversational learning that encourages and fosters catalytic conversations. These conversations help glean the organizational wisdom from the past to bring it forward to create more proactive, innovative futures. Through these interactions, people also learn from others' talents and experiences to see through their own blind spots and filters. By talking through misunderstandings, people can collectively discover new understandings.

Given how deeply embedded cultural norms are within institutions, cultural changes occur slowly. These institutions are often stabilizing forces and obstacles to change. It is important to honor the history and culture of organizations while proactively anticipating the future. In essence, by serving as a tether between the past and the future people want to create, catalytic conversations and conversational learning feed generative change processes that benefit organizations, employees, and other stakeholders. They help organizations hold onto the deep knowledge and wisdom they need and bring it forward to create the future they want. These conversations are also catalysts for ongoing organizational learning that is critical to adaptability, knowledge creation, and innovation.

References

Argyris, C. 1994. Good communication that blocks learning. *Harvard Business Review* July-August: 26–37.
———. 1997. *On organizational learning.* Oxford, UK: Blackwell Business.
Baker, A., P. Jensen, and D. Kolb. 2002. *Conversational learning: An experiential approach to knowledge creation.* Westport, CT: Quorum Books.
Barrett, M. 2004. Should they learn to interrupt? Workplace communication strategies Australian women managers forecast as effective. *Women in Management Review* 19 (7/8): 391–403.
Brown, J. S., and P. Duguid. 1991. Organizational learning and communities-of-practice: Toward a unified view of working, learning and innovation. *Organization Science* 2 (1): 40–57.
———. 2000. *The social life of organization.* Boston: Harvard Business School Press.
Burbules, N. C., and S. Rice. 1991. Dialogue across differences: Continuing the conversation. *Harvard Educational Review* 61 (4): 393–416.
Case, S. S. 1993. The collaborative advantage: The usefulness of women's language to contemporary business problems. *Business in a Contemporary World* 5 (3): 81–105.
Crawford, M. 1989. Humor in conversational contexts: Beyond biases in the study of gender and humor. In *Representations: Social constructions of gender,* ed. R. K. Unger, 155–166. Amityville, NY: Baywood.

Choo, C. W. 1998. *The knowing organization: How organizations use information to construct meaning, create knowledge, and make decisions.* New York: Oxford University Press.

Eisenhardt, K. M., J. L. Kahwajy, and L. J. Bourgeois III. 1997. Conflict and strategic choice: How top management teams disagree. *California Management Review* 39 (2): 42–62.

Engestrom, Y., and D. Middleton. 1996. *Cognition and communication at work.* Cambridge, UK: Cambridge University Press.

Fiumara, G. C. 1990. *The other side of language: A philosophy of listening.* New York: Routledge.

Frye, M. 2001. *Race, class and gender: An anthology.* 4th ed. Belmont, CA: Wadsworth: 48–52.

Fukuyama, F. 1995. *Trust: The social virtues and the creation of prosperity.* New York: Simon & Schuster.

Gersick, C. 1988. Time and transition in work teams: Toward a new model of group development. *Academy of Management Journal* 31 (1): 9–42.

Habermas, J. 1991. *Moral consciousness and communicative action.* Cambridge, MA: MIT Press.

Hampden-Turner, C. M., and F. Trompenaars. 1993. *The seven cultures of capitalism: Value systems for creating wealth in the United States, Japan, Germany, France, Britain, Sweden, and the Netherlands.* New York: Currency/Doubleday.

———. 2000. *Building cross-cultural competence: How to create wealth from conflicting values.* New Haven, CT: Yale University Press.

Henley, N. M., and C. Kramarae. 1991. Gender, power, and miscommunication. In *"Miscommunication" and problematic talk,* ed. N. Coupland, H. Giles, and J. M. Wiemann, Newbury Park, CA: Sage: 18–43.

Hofstede, G. 1991. *Cultures and organizations: Software of the mind.* New York: McGraw Hill.

Johnson, D. W., and R. T. Johnson. 1989. *Cooperation and competition: Theory and research.* Edina, MN: Interaction Books.

Kersten, A. 2000. Diversity management: Dialogue, dialectics and diversion. *Journal of Organizational Change Management* 13 (3): 235–248.

Krolokke, C., and A. S. Sorensen. 2006. *Gender communication theories and analyses: From silence to performance.* Thousand Oaks, CA: Sage.

Lewis, R. 1999. *When cultures collide: Managing successfully across cultures.* London: Nicholas Brealey Publishing.

Mathews, D. 1995. Building a strong civil society and a healthy public life. *Connections.* Dayton, OH: Kettering Foundation.

McIntosh, P. 2007. White privilege and male privilege: Unpacking the invisible knapsack. In *Race, class and gender: An anthology,* 6th ed., ed. L. Andersen and P. H. Collins. Belmont, CA: Thomson Wadsworth.

Miller, J. B. 1986. *Toward a new psychology of women.* Boston: Beacon Press.

Nonaka, I. 1994. A dynamic theory of organizational knowledge creation. *Organization Science* 5 (1): 14–37.

Nonaka, I., and H. Takeuchi. 1995. *The knowledge-creating company: How Japanese companies create the dynamics of innovation.* New York: Oxford University Press.

Pearce, W. B. 1995. Bringing news of difference: Participation in systemic social constructionist communication. In *Innovations in group facilitation: Applications in natural settings,* ed. L. R. Frey, 94–115. Cresskill, NJ: Hampton Press.

Richter, I. 1998. Individual and organizational learning at the executive level: Towards a research agenda. *Management Learning* 29 (3): 299–316.

Rycroft, R. W., and D. E. Kash. 1999. *The complexity challenge: Technological innovation for the 21st century.* New York: Pinter.

Schrage, M. 1990. *Shared minds: The new technologies of collaboration.* New York: Random House.

Shaw, P. 2002. *Changing conversations in organizations: A complexity approach to change.* New York: Routledge.

Thomas, D. A., and R. J. Ely. 1996. Making differences matter: A new paradigm for managing diversity. *Harvard Business Review* (September-October): 79–90.

Tjosvold, D., K. Law, S. Kenneth, and H. F. Sun. 2003. Collectivistic and individualistic values: Their effects on group dynamics and productivity in China. *Group Decision and Negotiation* 12: 243–263.

Tjosvold, D., and H. F. Sun. 2002. Understanding conflict avoidance: Relationship, motivations, actions, and consequences. *International Journal of Conflict Management* 13 (2): 142–164.

Williams, K. Y., and C. A. O'Reilly. 1998. Demography and diversity in organizations: A review of 40 years of research. *Research in Organizational Behavior* 20: 77–140.

Part II

5

Constructive Controversy and Intentional Conversation

When "... solving problems *as understood* is more useful than understanding them differently" (Reich 1988, 7), we forestall social learning. If the drive to reach a goal drowns out efforts to understand the larger context and background of the situation, we set ourselves up for treating symptoms and create a breeding ground for worse problems. Often people are reluctant to do the work necessary to find new ways of understanding because it takes time, requires openness to the unfamiliar, and requires skill to be able to encounter differences productively. Each of these challenges is formidable.

It can be a challenge to improve communication and work effectively with people who think, and perhaps look and sound, unusual. Learning how to engage in *constructive controversy* is a part of the answer. Constructive controversy is one way of setting generative change processes in motion. In constructive controversy, open-minded communication is intentional as people try to reach new understandings with one another.

Constructive controversy is "the open-minded discussion of diverse views" (Tjosvold, Law, and Sun 2003, 247). Being *open* involves intentional willingness to listen and consider the perspectives of those with differing views and to work through conflicts that erupt out of differences.

Intentional Conversation

Based upon meta-analyses of hundreds of studies on conflict (Johnson and Johnson 1989; Tjosvold 1998), it has been determined that "what is critical is how conflict partners believe the other is trying to deal with the conflict, more than the specific behaviours performed" (Tjosvold 1998, 304). The *intentions* that undergird engagements, words, and behaviors have a crucial effect. When people acknowledge differences and intend to try to learn, be constructive, and confront the conflict in that same spirit, controversy takes on a new character. *Intent* is the nexus between bringing differences into organizational conversations and benefiting from them.

In conflict, people's intentions and expectations influence how the conversation evolves (Argyris 1994, 1997; Eisenhardt, Kahwajy, and Bourgeois 1997; Simons, Pelled, and Smith 1999). People can try to work constructively with each other or they can avoid, ignore, delay, or overrun others. While these approaches can be described in various ways, Deutsch (cited in Johnson and Johnson 1989) identifies three basic paths to resolve conflict—cooperation, competition, and independence. Tjosvold (1998) similarly describes the different mind-sets of individuals when they are in conflict.

A competitive frame of reference is relatively easy to identify in individuals and groups who attempt to be the sole winner, because success requires overrunning or defeating others. In a cooperative frame of reference, the recognition of mutual interests, that is, goals, missions, purposes, consequences, long-term and short-term considerations, creates incentives for people to find constructive ways to work together. Research and practical experience indicate that "open discussion of opposing views is critical for making cooperative situations productive and enhancing" (Tjosvold 1998, 291). When the strategy is to delay or avoid the conflict, people's intentions are more ambiguous. To evaluate intentionality in these situations, much more specific information about a given context is required (Baker, Jensen, and Kolb 2002; Johnson and Johnson 1989; Tjosvold 1998; Tjosvold and Sun 2002; Tjosvold et al. 2003).

The work on knowledge creation, complexity, innovation, and learning organizations provides extensive evidence of the need for collaborative and cooperative relationships. At the core of this work, once again, is the importance of the intentions that people bring to the table and the organization's capacity for continuous learning through nonthreatening, constructive exploration of differences (Brown and Duguid 1991, 2000; Eisenhardt et al. 1997; Isaacs 1999; Nonaka 1994; Nonaka and Takeuchi 1995; Rycroft and Kash 1999; Wenger 1998).

Open-mindedness and constructive controversy are more feasible in supportive environments and relationships of trust. People may have the necessary skills and still find it difficult to be effective without an organizational environment that supports relationship building (Edmondson 1999, 1996). For example, rewards and incentive programs must be congruent. In fact, "considerable organizational change effort[s] . . . may be necessary to develop cooperative goals" (Tjosvold 1998, 304).

Conversational Learning

A receptive conversational learning environment facilitates constructive controversy. Experiences and relationships among people influence the language they use in the same way that the language and tone of voice influence what they hear and the meaning that they make in their conversations. When differences inflame people who then insist on trying to prove that they are right or that other people are wrong, it jeopardizes working relationships and sometimes involves the use of power to suppress others. The differences can take on a life of their own in positive and not-so-positive ways.

Bumping into differences can lead to curiosity (e.g., wanting to hear more, having a stream of questions, feeling surprised and inquisitive, being provoked to contemplate new possibilities, perceiving the differences as intriguing). Bumping into differences can lead to attraction (e.g., being drawn toward the complementarities that others offer, wanting more, liking the surprises, and feeling energized by the unfamiliar). Attraction to differences, of course, is a cogent facet of romantic relationships and certainly can be a part of any relationship. It can create more openness to the unfamiliar and can make work and life more fun.

On the other hand, bumping into differences can lead to avoidance (e.g., avoiding certain people, potential arguments, disagreeable things, feeling pressure to change, feelings of fear or anger). Bumping into differences can also lead to clashes that may erupt when people are expressing anger verbally or physically, standing up for beliefs, or trying to prove they are right.

On the surface, it may seem naïve to suggest that reframing perceptions and being intentional about how people talk to each other can have a weighty impact. Yet a fundamental organizational challenge is the urgency to find constructive ways to grapple with intense differences between individuals and groups of people. People must be able to disagree in ways that increase understanding and acceptance, rather than disagree in ways that repel. They must be able to use their conversations to work through the misunderstandings (Burbules and Rice 1991). People need to integrate their multiple interpretations to discover new knowledge together, which is the essence of conversational learning spaces that facilitate catalytic conversations (Baker et al. 2002).

Differences generate energy that can feel like an electrical charge. One aspect of using the energy in positive ways involves learning how to have "better conversations" without avoiding controversial differences. In skillful conversations, the differences become resources. William Isaacs (1999) says that we can use

> the energy of our differences . . . channeling it toward something that has never been created before. It lifts us out of polarization and into a greater common sense, and is thereby a means for accessing the intelligence and coordinated power of groups of people. (p.19)

Relationships between people and groups are at the heart of organizational and interorganizational dynamics as the participants continuously reorganize themselves (Addleson 2006). Ongoing relationships can provide the support needed when first testing the unfamiliar ground of learning to talk openly and constructively about differences. Another common element of conversational learning and constructive controversy is the fundamental assumption that the responsibility for learning and change rests with each participant in the conflict. There must be openness on all sides because

> [p]ublic deliberation works to foster changes in belief only when the persuaders on both sides subject themselves to opposing suasion, when the *wooer is willing to be wooed.* This active and passive art is not instinctive; it must be taught. (Heinrichs 1995, 42)

These characteristics are no less important in private deliberations.

The importance of being able and *willing to be wooed* is reinforced by Jean Baker Miller (1986), who says that "Growth requires engagement with difference and with people embodying that difference. If differences were more openly acknowledged, we could allow for, and even encourage, an increasingly strong expression by each party of her or his experience" (p. 13).

When people are open to iteratively hearing and learning from one another, a wide range of nuances can be uncovered and become more legitimate. They share information, ask questions, and give each other background, all of which makes it easier for individuals to develop fuller pictures of others. When they can reflect together and can consider one another's perspectives and experiences, it becomes easier to discover possibilities beyond the kind of dualistic thinking that focuses on determining who is right and who is wrong.

Innovation and the development of new alternatives depend on questioning assumptions and creating forums where ideas and differences can be openly shared (Brown and Duguid 1991, 2000; Eisenhardt 1997; Rycroft and Kash 1999; Wenger 1998). Listening to and welcoming perspectives that may be unexpected and uncomfortable is also essential, as is engaging with people in a spirit of trying to understand, trying to be understood, and trying to learn from one another (Baker 1995; Edmondson 1999, 1996). When understanding is primary, the manner in which people talk and listen is affected.

I want to emphasize that I am not suggesting a value-free process where any difference is acceptable. I am not advocating an *anything goes* attitude or *relativism*. I am suggesting that individuals have a responsibility to be open to the possibility that there are aspects of any issue that they do not understand. Everyone must be open to learning from words, ideas, and approaches that are unfamiliar and to the possibility that we can discover new horizons with others that we might not appreciate on our own (Baker et al. 2002; Gadamer 1994; Kimball and Garrison 1999). In this context, our horizons are a metaphor for how far and how clearly we can learn to see. For example, if I describe my interpretation of an experience you could say that my horizon is this particular interpretation, with its unique insights and limitations. However, if we then talk about the experience I described and others that are relevant, as you share your perspectives it is possible that my horizon could extend far beyond where it was originally. This would be the result of the new aspects that I had not originally considered. It is possible that together we would create new knowledge and insight that neither of us had previously realized. When our horizons are limited only to familiar or traditional frames of reference, we must have conversations that provoke catalysts to jolt us out of unconscious habits. When these processes are set in motion and supported, people more readily engage in constructive controversy.

Conflict: Differences That Matter and Differences That Don't

Both the everyday and the extraordinary events of life involve vast interactions. The focus of attention for one person may not be impor-

Figure 5.1a **Boundary perceptions: similarities and differences**

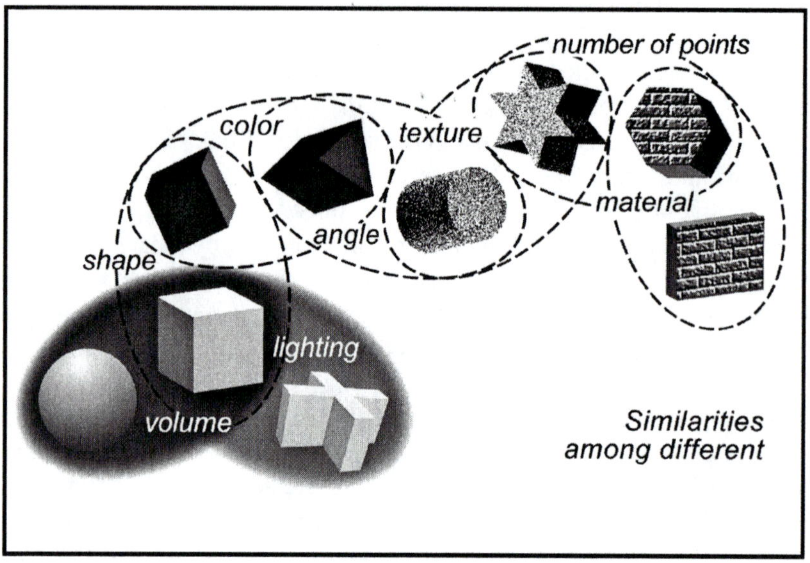

tant to another, so there must be enough similarity or connection for something to grasp our attention and become interesting. Without difference, boredom sets in, and it is hard to stay engaged. "We need to be similar enough to make dialogue possible, but we also need to be different enough to make it worthwhile" (Burbules and Rice 1991, 17). Figure 5.1a illustrates boundary perceptions from the point of view of similarities among differences.

Another way to think about this dynamic is to consider the relative proportions of likeness and unlikeness. The more similarities there are, the more the differences stand out. For instance, there are so few ways that a plant and a house are alike, rarely would someone pay much attention to the ways that they are unlike each other. On the other hand, the similarities between maple trees and oak trees are interesting to a variety of people, such as a naturalist on a hike, a gardener, or a botanist. The preponderance of shared characteristics of trees heightens interest in their differences. Overlapping likenesses attract attention (see Figure 5.1b).

Understanding the interplay between likeness and unlikeness offers insight into sources of organizational tension. These tensions reflect both the interests of the participants and the pressures and influences of

Figure 5.1b   **Boundary perceptions: similarities and differences**

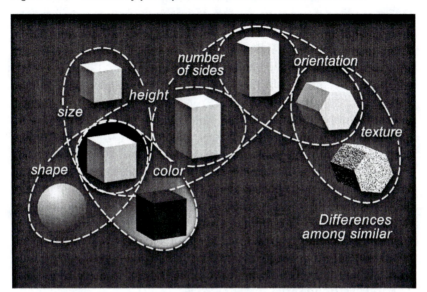

the outside world. Consider two conscientious professionals, whom I will call Jim and John: With several important new projects beginning, their organization assigns them to work collaboratively as co-leaders of a project team. Each of them has a reputation as bright, responsible, and hardworking. They begin their work together with expectations of success. As their project develops, it becomes apparent that Jim thinks the success of the project depends on close, directive leadership. To achieve high quality and quick results, he wants the two of them to be decisive and direct others to perform as needed. However, partially because this project has widespread implications for people throughout the organization, John thinks it is important for as many people as possible to have input into the planning and decision-making process, while also fully supporting the need to complete the work within the required time frame. When Jim and John discover their strong differences, their previous assumptions about their similarities intensify tensions that lead to conflict. If they can reinforce each other's strengths and commitments, they can talk openly, which provides openings for them to discover common ground. They can use their similarities as a foundation upon which they can engage in constructive controversy.

Another example of the interplay between similarity and differences is found in devout members of different sects within the same religion. Often such groups are unable to accept one another's differences. Their similarities at least partially sharpen explosive reactions to these differences—e.g., Catholics and Protestants in Ireland; Shiite and Sunni Muslims in Iraq; Orthodox and Reform in the Middle East. Of course, there are other sources of these conflicts, but it also seems as though their similar religious foundations set up expectations that narrow the range of acceptability for interpretations and beliefs that deviate from their own. Expectations associated with similarities of beliefs and values make the differences in interpretations and associated rituals even more intensely noticeable. The ways that they are different take on more meaning than if there was no expectation of commonality. When the expectations are to find similarity, the fundamental differences seem to surprise, and tensions build quickly. It is much more difficult to turn this pattern around once it begins than to prevent it, and this is a critical lesson for organizations to incorporate.

The Illusive Boundaries of Categories

The capacity for flexibility and openness also relates to the perceptions about the boundaries between and within organizations. As in the two earlier, rigid boundaries make it more difficult to move or stretch to learn and reshape perceptions. If people and groups perceive their boundaries as porous and flexible, they seem more likely to be able to try out new frames of reference, to move into more overlapping relationships, and to see through their boundaries to develop mutual respect and common ground. To illustrate, I will describe three types of boundaries that are especially relevant to organizational communication: boundaries between similarities and dissimilarities, boundaries between self and group identity, and context boundaries. As people work across differences, perceptions of these boundaries influence the capacity for openness to new learning.

The boundaries between similarities and dissimilarities define categories within organizations. The categories create a perception of groups as being different from each other. While labels can be used to identify groups and facilitate communication and convey meaning concisely, labels can also become a way of categorizing people (e.g., people of color vs. whites, well-educated vs. uneducated, Muslim vs. Christian, liberal vs. conservative). Although these labels, names, and theories about different groups provide handy shortcuts to say a lot in few words, they mean different things to different people and thus are often misleading and can lead to misunderstandings. For example, when a person is described as a liberal or a conservative, the intended meaning may be clear to the speaker and yet may conjure up wholly different images and associations to the listener—creating reactions, miscommunications, and misunderstandings. When used carelessly, such words easily become stereotypes that convey incorrect meanings that are even more problematic.

Part of human development involves incorporating particular groups into one's sense of identity and into self-perceptions. A person engages in a process of self-identification (figuring out who I am). Simultaneously, a person identifies with groups in his or her own social milieu (who am I in relation to the world around me, both near and far). These processes of individual and social identification are interdependent and thus always influence each other. The language used (the way we talk) to categorize people often does not adequately take into account the "active processes of group identification and . . . subjectivity. To put it simply, there are differences we choose and differences we do not choose" (Burbules and Rice 1991, 400). In other words, people tend to categorize each other as immutable, sometimes one-dimensional, assigning others to one group or another and thus attributing to them more or less status or influence. However, each individual's sense of identity is in flux as time passes. For example, a person may identify strongly with being an athlete through high school and college. Later in life, school friends may still think of this person first as an athlete while the person's self-identify may have shifted to more current roles such as a professional identity or that of father or mother (see Figure 5.2).

When we have close affinity with a group, characteristics of that group naturally matter more to us. For example, although I drive a car a lot, when I hear critical comments about drivers, criticism about the group does not bother me because drivers are not a group with which I strongly identify. On the other hand, being a woman is important to my sense of self, and I identify strongly with womankind as a group. Consequently, when I encounter derogatory perspectives or attitudes toward women, I notice them immediately and pay especially close attention. The more strongly people identify with a group, the more rigid and inflexible are their likely perceptions of the boundaries that distinguish that group from others. Thus, a challenge in working across differences is for people to

Figure 5.2 **Boundary perceptions: group and self-identification**

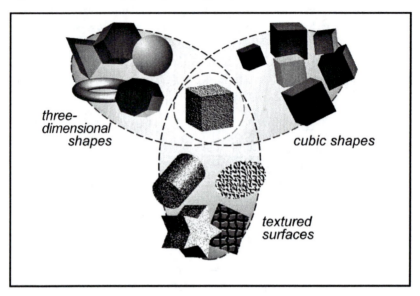

become more flexible and at the same time not lose their own sense of self, values, and beliefs.

A third kind of boundary perception that influences the capacity to work across boundaries is context. Whether differences matter to us and how strongly we identify with certain groups varies from one context to another. For example, if two men who work in the same organization meet, their physical differences may or may not matter. It will depend on the circumstances related to their meeting. For instance, if one man is much taller, the difference in height may or may not matter, depending at least partially on the context. If the reason they meet is clear, focused, and has nothing to do with physical attributes, as when one man who is a computer expert arrives to try to bring the other man's crashed computer back online, the height difference is unlikely to be given much thought. Instead, their shared focus is the task. If, on the other hand, these two men meet because they will be working as partners on rescue missions, the difference in height can take on perhaps exaggerated prominence (see Figure 5.3).

Another aspect of contextual influence relates to the limitations of any label or category. Labels only describe one of the many facets of who a person or a group is. For example, I am a woman, mother, daughter,

Figure 5.3   **Boundary perceptions: contextual influence**

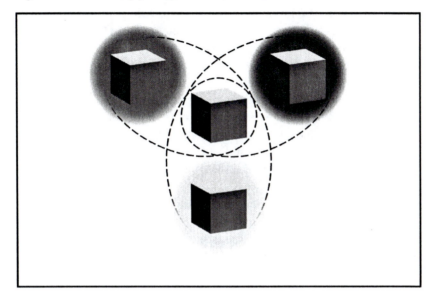

citizen of the United States, and far more all at the same time. Within each of these groups, there are vast differences limiting the applicability of any generalized description. Rarely are characterizations of women acceptable to all women; rarely are characterizations of mothers acceptable to all mothers, and so on. Multiple identities sharply demonstrate the complexity of differences and the limitations of making assumptions based on a category. In fact, Hanrahan (2000, 122) describes complexity by saying,

> Dynamic cultural processes tend to produce difference in . . . existing social and cultural categories. . . . There are in fact *multiple possible relations* between the parts and therefore no fixed boundaries between categories of difference. That is the definition of complexity." (Emphasis added)

In complex systems, the *multiple possible relations* exist as overlapping descriptors. With more porous boundaries, people are better able to negotiate and renegotiate multiple roles through their relationships and conversations.

To add further to this maze of influences, there are many exceptions to all of these patterns. Individuals or groups of each culture adhere to norms unevenly. Global media and communication, the Internet, travel, and global commerce influence cultural norms across political boundaries more than ever before. Although they change slowly, even cultural norms are not static, because perceptions are always fluid and evolving. Although it may be useful at times to use broad descriptions, generalized characterizations overlook the complexity and fluidity of context, culture, and changing self and group identifications. When boundaries are porous, working together in constructive controversy is easier. At the same time, having a clear sense of boundaries gives a person or a group a firmer sense of who they are and can help them feel less threatened as they renegotiate ongoing relationships.

Conflict in Cross-cultural Contexts

Cultural norms about conflict function much like category boundaries. There are specific cross-cultural norms that influence the usefulness of constructive controversy and the likelihood of having catalytic conversations across cultural contexts. The contrasting patterns between collectivist norms that are more common in the East and individualistic norms more typically associated with the West are especially relevant. The following are a few examples for illustration.

The Chinese culture in particular has ancient traditions of resolving conflicts through processes that emphasize the well-being of the community as a whole, giving less importance to the interests of individuals. Given these broad norms, it would be reasonable to suppose that the Chinese would be less inclined to talk directly about differing views given their focus on the community, their preference for substantive decision making outside of the public eye, and the importance of saving face. Perhaps people in the East avoid conflict more than in the West because of collectivist norms, thus making it more difficult to work through differences.

Recent research provides evidence to the contrary. Based on a series of studies, it appears that in China and Hong Kong "collectivist values promote relationships . . . not through avoidance [of conflict] but through the direct, constructive discussions of different viewpoints" (Tjosvold et al. 2003, 255). Because of the strong emphasis on building and maintaining relationships, people may actually be more able to engage in the kind of constructive conflict management than is typical in more individualistic cultures. Perhaps talking openly about their differences may not seem as threatening to the Chinese because of the emphasis on building strong relationships. I also speculate that given the prevailing cultural norms for saving face and showing respect in the East, people are more comfortable talking openly about their differences because they are less concerned about ridicule and embarrassment in front of others.

On the other hand, in China and Hong Kong individualistic behavior seems to be growing to some extent, perhaps from global influences. According to one study, the more these cultures embrace individualism, "the more [people in conflict] were close-minded to various perspectives and less productive" (Tjosvold et al. 2003, 255). Perhaps as more individualistic behaviors such as efficiency and straightforward communication receive more attention and building relationships receives less emphasis, people are more concerned about embarrassment. In the United States, at least partially because they cannot assume respectful interactions, people are often less inclined to talk openly about their differences (Argyris 1994, 1997; Edmonson 1996, 1999).

Another intriguing study (Peng and Nisbett 1999) looked at possible differences between the ways in which European Americans and Chinese cope with contradictions, which are often at the heart of conflict. Researchers asked the participants to respond to proverbs and vignettes that posed contradictions, such as contradictory research on global warming or healthy diets. When faced with contradictions, the Euro-American participants were inclined to choose one side of the contradiction as right and the other as wrong. In contrast, Chinese participants were much more comfortable allowing for the possibility "that both sides of a contradiction might be right and that the truth lies between the two perspectives" (Peng and Nisbett 1999, 749). Accepting more ambiguity may facilitate recognition of the complexity of contradictions.

Another relevant finding relates to cultural differences in the tendency to see an object or person as a part of a larger context or to isolate and separate it from the context. According to some research, Euro-Americans were more predisposed to see objects separate from their larger context (Hampden-Turner and Trompenaars 2000; Kaufman 1995; Peng and Nisbett 1999; Waldrop 1992). They stripped away the context rather than using the approach that the Chinese were more likely to take when they considered the object as a part of a larger context or picture. In other words, the Chinese tended to consider the broader context, which encompassed more complexity. In essence, the Euro-Americans' inclination to find a right and a wrong answer depends upon stripping away the context of the situation; and that, in turn, oversimplifies the dilemma. This tendency to polarize issues and therefore strip away related contextual information to determine a correct answer is consistent with the logical, linear approach that "may be optimal for scientific exploration and the search for facts" (Peng and Nisbett 1999, 751). On the other hand, the Chinese "reasoning may be preferable for intelligently negotiating in complex social interactions" (Peng and Nisbett 1999, 751).

A focus on broader contexts and holding open the possibility for multiple perspectives in diverse complex environments with conflicting data and varied perspectives is more common in the East. When there is more focus on the whole than on isolated parts of an issue, people in conflict become more aware of their interdependence as they try to cooperate. By talking calmly and considering situations from multiple perspectives, it is easier to take into account a wider range of alternatives, which is the essence of constructive controversy (Baker et al. 2002; Kimball and Garrison 1999). Because of the need to work "intelligently in complex social interactions," I agree with Peng and Nisbett (1999) that "ideal thought tendencies might be a combination of . . . the synthesis . . . of Eastern and Western ways of thinking" (p. 751). While these studies are not conclusive, this research demonstrates how critical it is to understand more about culturally diverse interaction patterns in conflict situations.

Chapter 6 builds on the idea of learning how to engage in constructive controversy by developing a better understanding of the importance of the conversational context to help people learn from each other.

References

Addleson, M. 2006. Learning organizations: The emergence of a relational-interpretive view of organization. In *The social construction of organization,* ed. D. M. Hosking and S. McNamee, 196–207. Oslo: Liber.

Argyris, C. 1994. Good communication that blocks learning. *Harvard Business Review* (July-August): 26–37.

———. 1997. *On organizational learning.* Oxford, UK: Blackwell Business.

Baker, A. C. 1995. Bridging differences and learning through conversation. Published dissertation.

Baker, A. C., P. Jensen, and D. Kolb. 2002. *Conversational learning: An experiential approach to knowledge creation.* Westport, CT: Quorum Books.

Brown, J. S., and P. Duguid. 1991. Organizational learning and communities-of-practice: Toward a unified view of working, learning and innovation. *Organization Science* 2 (1): 40–57.

———. 2000. *The social life of organization.* Boston: Harvard Business School Press.

Burbules, N. C., and S. Rice. 1991. Dialogue across differences: Continuing the conversation. *Harvard Educational Review* 61 (4): 393–416.

Edmondson, A. 1996. Learning from mistakes is easier said than done: Group and organizational influences on the detection and correction of human error. *Journal of Applied Behavioral Science* 32: 5–28.

———. 1999. Psychological safety and learning behavior. *Administrative Science Quarterly* 44: 350–383.

Eisenhardt, K. M., J. L. Kahwajy, and L. J. Bourgeois, III. 1997. Conflict and strategic choice: How top management teams disagree. *California Management Review* 39 (2): 42–62.

Gadamer, H. G. 1994. *Truth and method.* 2d rev. ed. New York: Crossroad.

Hampden-Turner, C. M., and F. Trompenaars. 2000. *Building cross-cultural competence: How to create wealth from conflicting values.* New Haven, CT: Yale University Press.

Hanrahan, N. W. 2000. *Difference in time: A critical theory of culture.* Westport, CT: Praeger.

Heinrichs, J. 1995. How Harvard destroyed rhetoric. *Harvard Magazine* (July-August): 37–42.

Isaacs, W. 1999. *Dialogue and the art of thinking together.* New York: Currency.

Johnson, D. W., and R. T. Johnson. 1989. *Cooperation and competition: Theory and research.* Edina, MN: Interaction Books.

Kauffman, S. 1995. *At home in the universe: The search for the laws of self-organization and complexity.* New York: Oxford University Press.

Kimball, S. L., and J. Garrison. 1999. Hermeneutic listening in multicultural conversations. In *Affirming diversity through democratic conversations,* ed. V. R. Fu and A. J. Stremmel, 5–27. Upper Saddle River, NJ: Merrill.

Miller, J. B. 1986. *Toward a new psychology of women.* Boston: Beacon Press.

Nonaka, I. 1994. A dynamic theory of organizational knowledge creation. *Organization Science* 5 (1): 14–37.

Nonaka, I., and H. Takeuchi. 1995. *The knowledge-creating company: How Japanese companies create the dynamics of innovation.* New York: Oxford University Press.

Peng, K., and R. E. Nisbett. 1999. Culture, dialectics, and reasoning about contradiction. *American Psychologist* 54 (9): 741–754.

Reich, R. 1988. *The power of public ideas.* Cambridge, Mass: Harvard University Press.

Rycroft, R. W., and D. E. Kash. 1999. *The complexity challenge: Technological innovation for the 21st Century.* New York: Pinter.

Simons, T., L. H. Pelled, and K. A. Smith. 1999. Making use of difference: Diversity, debate, and decision comprehensiveness in top management teams. *Academy of Management Journal* 42 (6): 662–673.

Tjosvold, D. 1998. Cooperative and competitive goal approach to conflict: Accomplishments and challenges. *Applied Psychology: An International Review* 47 (3): 285–342.

Tjosvold, D., and H. F. Sun. 2002. Understanding conflict avoidance: Relationship, motivations, actions, and consequences. *International Journal of Conflict Management* 13 (2): 142–165.

Tjosvold, D., K. S. Law, and H. F. Sun. 2003. Collectivistic and individualistic values: Their effects on group dynamics and productivity in China. *Group Decision and Negotiation* 12: 243–263.

Waldrop, M. 1992. *Complexity: The emerging science at the edge of order and chaos.* New York: Touchstone.

Wenger, E. 1998. *Communities of practice: Learning, meaning, and identity.* New York: Cambridge University Press.

6

The Conversational Environment

Help or Hindrance?

The conversational environment is both a help and a hindrance to the quality of organizational communication. The leverage it potentially offers and the problems it may create are hard to exaggerate. Even though promoting an environment conducive to constructive conversations is a relatively inexpensive organizational investment, it is an atypical investment in most settings. This chapter addresses the profound power of attending to conversational spaces to enhance organizational communication, as does Chapter 7, which focuses on virtual conversations.

Conversational Space

People enact personal and work lives largely through conversations and behaviors that take place within particular *spaces, environments, contexts, mediums, webs*.[1] Visualizing the vast array of organizational conversations as elaborate spiderwebs within dense forests allows complex, overlapping contexts to take more concrete form.

The interactions and conversations that occur in organizations must be understood in relation to the spaces in which they occur. Indeed, they are inseparable from them. They emerge out of social life and its specific structural, historical, and relational circumstances while also shaping and transforming the social life.[2] One must likewise consider that there are also interpersonal, cultural, task-related, and psychological dimensions to social life.

Conversational space is a topic of interest among diverse writers and practitioners who refer to it using various names: a knowledge space (von Krogh, Ichijo, and Nonaka 2000), container (Isaacs 1999), receptive space (Baker 1995; Baker, Jensen, and Kolb 2002), holding environment (Winnicott 1992), and the social embodiment of experiential learning (Baker et al. 2002). There are also both microlevel dimensions of space

Figure 6.1 **The precourse, discourse, and post-course dialectic in conversation**

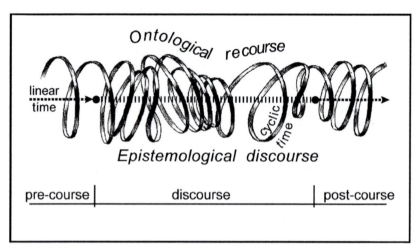

among the people communicating, such as relationships and trust, and macrolevel elements, such as broader cultural structures and patterns. While this chapter devotes more attention to the microlevel, several macrolevel influences are also addressed. The common thread that runs through all of them is the significance of the context and the influence it has on people and their conversations.

The environment within which a conversation occurs is created long before anyone speaks. Previous conversations (i.e., pre-course) influence the sense that people make of and take away from conversations as well as the subsequent interactions (i.e., post-course) that follows (see Figure 6.1). Conversations are affected by participants' expectations, fears, biases, and cultural backgrounds; group norms; preceding events and nonevents; and physical or virtual spaces where conversations occur. The purpose of the conversations is also critical. Some are direct, decisive, and linear, and the focus is on closure, while others are exploratory, meandering, and inquisitive.

Swirling around even the most linear conversations however are others that confuse, elaborate, develop, and return to similar topics or themes (i.e., recursive conversations) as people continuously try to make sense of their organizational lives (Figure 6.1). In this way, threads of conversation occur over time and link with earlier conversations, influencing future conversations as well.

Cultural patterns distinctly influence perceptions of space. One general cultural predilection in Eastern cultures (Hall 1966) is to *see* and be attuned to the space that *surrounds* objects, as opposed to the Western tendency to focus on the *objects within* the space and to think of the surrounding space as being *empty*. One way to illustrate the distinction is to imagine you are using a camera. As you focus on a specific object, such as a flower or animal, you bring that object into sharp clarity within its larger background. On the other hand, when more attuned to the environment surrounding the object, such as a garden or a forest, the focus changes. It shifts to the *space* that holds the objects in a field that varies in depth.

It is a bit of a paradox to pay attention either to the space (the overall picture) *or* to the objects within the space (only parts of the picture). The capacity to see and focus on combinations of space and objects of various depths presents genuine challenges, partially because cultural screening patterns function as coping strategies to manage countless stimuli. Yet the paradoxical perspectives are complementary. A flower, in a garden, in the bouquet of a bride, or on a casket in a funeral service tells vastly different stories. The *invisible* space, or context, shapes the social construction of the meaning that people make of the flower and the story it tells. The context that surrounds the flower is indispensable to making sense of its relevance in a given setting. Without paying attention to the surrounding space (i.e., the context), stories and meanings can be misunderstood. A lack of astute awareness of surrounding contexts leads an individual to miss or misunderstand webs of conversation and limits the vitality of an organization's potential. For instance, by focusing too much on a leader when working with an organization for the first time, it is easy to miss clues that either reinforce or contradict that person. It would be like reading only a small portion of available background material prior to beginning work on a project instead of preparing more fully.

Conversations about Differences

Within an organization, differences may include perspectives, expertise, experience, education, training, background, and culture (Schein 2004). Whether people can talk about difficult issues and disagree respectfully influences how they deal with their differences. The space within which conversations occur has a profound effect on whether differences can be *integrated* to promote learning and innovation, whether the differences are *avoided* altogether, or whether winner-takes-all tactics prevail. When stakeholders do not feel comfortable having conversations, the tendency is avoidance. These avoided topics are similar to what Argyris (1994) calls the *undiscussables* that quash opportunities to change unproductive patterns of interactions. Cogent concerns get swept under the proverbial rug, opportunities to learn from differences are lost, misunderstandings continue and fester, and negative feelings grow.

I encountered a similar instance when a CEO proposed a broad, cutting-edge project that would change the organization. Even though the CEO initially sought and considered questions and differences, he did not have the patience to remain engaged and thus declared an implementation plan and assigned duties. The result was increased resistance to change. Some of the key implementers, while technically following the CEO's orders, deliberately undermined the overall effort by subtly narrowing the scope, thus minimizing the potential for substantial change. By rushing to implementation, the CEO in essence made the differences *undiscussables,* thus ultimately sabotaging his own innovative efforts.

In contrast, in an environment that promotes *conversational learning,* people can transform their collective experiences and differences into new knowledge through the sense they make together. Esther Wyss-Flamm's model of conversational learning (Figure 6.2) in multicultural teams is instructive here. When people disagree and differences surface in a conversation, the differences become part of the social experience among the participants.

Sometimes the differences draw a lot of attention while people quickly drop them at other times. If the differences continue to be a part of the conversation, a juxtaposition of the intersecting, divergent perspectives occurs. Wyss-Flamm's work (2003 a, 2003b) suggests that although there are cultural differences in how groups proceed, when participants contend with their differences, they typically use one of two patterns.

At the conversational juxtaposition, people either *integrate* the differences into the conversation, and hence into their understandings, or they *resolve* them. If the group asserts the contrast without hearing alternatives, *resolution* comes when "one side of the tension . . . [is] declared correct while the other is dismissed as flawed or wrong" (p. 157). Learning and negotiation are blocked. The resolution produces winner(s) and loser(s) through an *either/or* resolution of the conflict.

On the other hand, *integrating* the differences sparks learning and for-

Figure 6.2 **Model of differences in conversational learning**

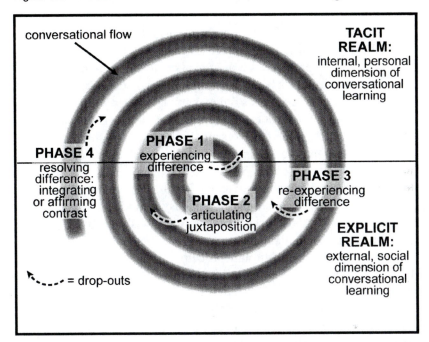

ward movement. Integrating differences "implies . . . letting go of one's own firmly held perspective cultivating one's ability to see a situation through new eyes . . . opening up and entering other ways of seeing" (p. 156). The integrative approach involves incorporating *both/and* options as distinct from making *either/or* choices. The both/and approach is a conversational learning mode in which people explore their differences and extend their potential for learning. Conversely, declaring that one side or the other is correct, as in the paragraph above, rather than continuing to strive for increased understanding is not conversational learning and is not engaging in catalytic conversations.

The passage of time and external pressures mean that changes are inevitable. Some managers also frequently change processes, objectives, and priorities without taking the time to assess progress and gather input, thereby further accelerating the preponderance of unpredictability. Regardless of whether people integrate, contrast, or avoid differences, the conversational contexts are dynamic, emergent, and impossible to control. Learning how to function in such dynamic environments is essential. At the same time, there must be enough flexibility for responsible adaptations.

Given current demographics and increasingly knowledge-intensive work, differences will rapidly increase in organizational life. The ambiguity and lack of predictability in global economies and organizations can be uncomfortable at best and terrifying at worst. "More than half of the GDP in the rich economies is now knowledge-based . . . Knowledge workers [now] account for eight out of ten new jobs" (Dess and Picken, 2000: 18). Already most managers are ill-prepared to facilitate the dense communication networks upon which knowledge workers depend. Rarely do educational and training programs adequately prepare people to work effectively in ambiguous environments or to use differences constructively in conversation. Nor is it easy for individuals, groups, or organizations to do their best work if they cannot ask questions, disagree, or influence decision making.

If an organizational environment seems stable over time, a real challenge for effective stakeholders is to avoid being lulled into trusting that stability. If the landscape seems too calm, it is better to seek more input because the stakeholders may be missing critical elements. For example, in a staff meeting where everyone agrees without question to a new directive given by the manager, it may be tempting for the manager to assume that silence means everyone supports the project. However, the silence may indicate fear, confusion, or resistance and be a sign of upcoming delays or impending efforts to undermine the project.

Furthermore, traditional economic, management, and business models exclude complex influences and isolate variables that interfere with certainty or predictability. In so doing, the models are seldom useful in twenty-first century organizational life where workers have to function in complex and ambiguous settings. In the contemporary world, the emphasis has to shift from certainty and predictability to *congruence*.

Congruence and Contradiction

In group, organizational, and interorganizational settings where complexity and rapid change are the norm, distinguishing between congruity and incongruity is more relevant than searching for the *right* answer or whom to blame. When words and behavior are congruent, the authenticity of the environment is palpable.

Consequently, there must be congruence between broad messages and daily behavior. Argyris (1994, 1997) describes it as congruence between an organization's *espoused theories* and its *theories-in-use.* In other words, is there congruence between the principles and values expressed and the actual behaviors? Does incongruence and contradiction seep into patterns of interaction and work relationships? Do people act on their speech (walk the talk) or not?

The capacity to walk the talk comes to life through congruence rather than in speeches and mission statements. Congruence grows out of clear intentions and shared visions continuously shaped and reshaped through diverse input. A person cannot mandate congruence because it is felt from deep inside rather than dictated from outside.

Congruity between what people say and do generates trustworthiness. For example, bosses who say they care about their employees like family earn trust through practice rather than by proclamation. Even when organizations let people go or even downsize, it is the *how* that determines congruence or incongruence. When people are fired suddenly, offered no transitional support, and allowed little face-saving, messages of "we are a family" are contradictory and breed cynicism. On the other hand, when people are given clear feedback and opportunities to improve and are counseled into transitioning out of the organization over time, congruity with the "family" talk is still possible. Credibility, relationships, and trust are undermined when words contradict the behavior.

At the macrolevel, organizational procedures and reward systems likewise must be congruent. For instance, when people are encouraged to be innovative, think outside of the box, and take risks, what is the organization's response when the risk taking does not lead to success? If it is punished, if the risk takers are publicly embarrassed or criticized, the incongruity between the message and the behavior seeps into the psyches of the people and the work environment. People hear the words and experience the incongruence.

Another example is when people are encouraged to cooperate and collaborate in cross-functional teams, and yet the organizational reward structure continues primarily to incentivize competition and individual achievement. The incongruity is full of contradiction that stakeholders experience even when they do not articulate it and may be unconscious of it. In turn, such incongruity breeds cynicism that undermines people's commitments to one another and to the organization. The challenge therefore is to create more congruent organizational environments to support the verbalized priorities, values, and mission. These environments in turn reinforce dedication to the superordinate values of the organization as a whole. No one can *design* this environment, though organizations can *design for* it (Jacobs and Heracleous 2005). Building the environment includes organizational investment in designing for catalytic conversations and conversational learning as "conversational learning cannot exist without a receptive space to hold it" (Baker, Jensen, and Kolb 2005, 424).

A one-size-fits-all conversational space is not the answer. Rather than following a fixed set of steps to support constructive conversation, organizations must dig much deeper to foster the emergence of conversational spaces that are congruent with their purpose, employees, clientele, and leadership. To chip away at existing incongruity, people must be able to talk through their differences in ways that are appropriate in that context. In turn, stakeholders' commitments to their decisions and ongoing relationships strengthen the environment.

This phenomenon is analogous to the difference between just knowing the kind of experience you and your traveling companions want to have on a trip and having an itinerary that fills in the details. The *collaborative* planning and itinerary building are interdependent, and yet no one can make a good trip happen. Having an image of the experience you want and planning how to travel can help you realize the image. For example, it is important to take the time to generate an image for yourself and your traveling companions as well as integrating their responses. What are the possible modes of travel? What are the time constraints, and how do they influence whether a car, boat, train, plane, or other travel mode is preferable? Are there financial resources to support the preferred mode? Are there fears that influence travel preferences, such as fear of flying or getting carsick in the mountains? The answer is, "it depends." It depends on the people going, the circumstances, the timing, the purpose—the context. Planning the trip is largely about *designing for* a shared context that is most likely to foster the preferred experience. It involves giving more priority to *congruence* than to doing it the *right* way, your way, or the way you have always done it before.

How does this analogy apply to organizations? We must intentionally create organizational contexts. They need to be congruent with and not contradict the organizational purposes and the people involved. The context must continuously integrate and reintegrate the inherent diversities. The integrity of authenticity and congruity provides potent resources for weathering and thriving in changing, ambiguous situations.

It can encourage people to work together for the constructive welfare of diverse stakeholders over the long term. The power of the integrity of congruence is immeasurable. It reflects the value of fostering working conversational contexts congruent with the organization, its stakeholders, and the nature of the work.

Nature of the Space

Paying careful attention to the context is analogous to what Nonaka (1994) describes as "'organization-wide' enabling conditions that promote a more favorable climate for effective knowledge creation" (p. 27). Nonaka singles out two necessary organizational conditions that enable people to discover new knowledge and understanding:

- To promote a climate of mutual trust
- To promote continuous, ongoing dialogue

Let's look at each of these enabling conditions, followed by a few more that I propose.

Mutual Trust

Trust is not just a good feeling about someone or a group. The *Oxford English Dictionary* (2nd edition) gives the following as the first definition of *trust*: "Confidence in or reliance on some quality or attribute of a person or thing, or the truth of a statement." The dictionary states that people can trust *in, of, on, upon, to,* and *unto.* Thus, trust is a mutual relationship built, earned, and maintained with others over time. Although trust can be broken in a moment, the rebuilding of trust requires considerable time and effort. Yet trust is not dependent on perfection. Mortals err. Instead, at the heart of trusting relationships are good intentions and genuine effort. In trusting relationships, people give each other the benefit of the doubt.

Ongoing Dialogue

Ongoing dialogue is the medium through which people work through differences, shortcomings, mistakes, and misunderstandings. When people err or misunderstand and do not talk through their thorny concerns, deterioration is set into motion. It is at this juncture that Nonaka's two conditions come together.

Within groups and organizations, the conversational space promotes or undermines trust and dialogue. In organizational studies, research on psychological safety and knowledge creation provides solid confirmation about the important role of organizational environment (Baker et al. 2002; Brown and Duguid 2000; Edmondson 1999; Jacobs and Heracleous 2005). The psychological safety research reiterates the tight links among people taking risks, creating knowledge, trusting colleagues, and exploring differences. It is through conversations that people learn whether they can trust each other and whether they feel psychologically safe.

Psychological safety has multiple dimensions, some of which vary culturally. Generally, people need some degree of mutual trust, strong relationships, nonjudgmental behavior, and benefit of the doubt, especially when conflicts and differences emerge. Receptive spaces must be prepared and held open to promote ongoing dialogue that includes surfacing differences (Baker 2002; Edmondson 1999). The space must be engaging enough for people to "suspend their view . . . [to] become willing to loosen the 'grip of certainty' about all views, including their own" (Isaacs 1993, 35).

Other Enabling Conditions

In addition to Nonaka's two enabling conditions, I suggest the following:

- time
- reflection
- norms
- boundaries

First, one's perspective of *time* is a crucial aspect of space. Time is an element of space that shapes the quality of interactions and makes a difference vis-à-vis alignment with organizations' evolving purposes and values. When efficiency is a centerpiece, when short-term results are the primary scale used for measuring success, when busyness is imperative, people perceive of time as scarce. It is an entity perceived to be rapidly used up. Enabling conditions are not congruent with the interpretation of time being continuously scarce. In an enabling space, the tension between *losing* the time and *taking* the time is held in some degree of balance to prevent either from dominating.

Perceptions of time and *reflection* are inextricably interdependent. By reflecting on events, conversations, and work, the opportunities to learn from them expand. Reflection on one's own successes and mistakes, satisfactions and frustrations, and habits and resistances fosters individual learning. For most people, it is difficult to be fully in a conversation and be consciously aware of the self, especially when the pace is fast and there is conflict. When in the midst of these situations, it is challenging to see one's own role in the conflict and be open to hearing other perspectives. Stepping back to reflect, however, can facilitate awareness of what is happening in the conversational space.

Schon (1983) articulated this dynamic in his work on the reflective practitioner. He said that each situation is a source of data and provides information. He suggested that one should become an astute observer of one's practices and to listen to discover what the situation reveals. He encouraged practitioners to pay attention to the *situation's talk-back*. For example, recognizing a group's resistance as feedback, rather than as a problem to suppress, reframes the perception of resistance. When a group is compliant, it is easy to assume agreement or success. But compliance is just another form of feedback and data. It is a source of information (Baker 2002; Block 2000; Schon 1983). The challenge is to discover the unique qualities of the situation and take the time to learn as it is *talking back*.

Collective reflection with others brings entirely new dimensions to learning and the potential to create new knowledge. When one person shares challenges, collective group knowledge emerges as others talk about how they worked through similar situations. The group can also brainstorm new ways to see troubling situations, tap new resources, and try new alternatives. As one person is able to trust the group enough to acknowledge shortcomings, to ask questions and ask for help, the group members' responses either encourage or discourage others to follow suit. If psychological safety builds, people gain confidence that they will not be embarrassed and humiliated by others in the group if they also ask for assistance. Team members learn to work together more effectively when they can ask for help and make unintentional mistakes without fear of embarrassment or retribution (Edmondson 1996, 1999). These behaviors especially facilitate team learning and the sharing of collective resources. Stronger relationships, increased engagement, and improved self-confidence are spin-off benefits of the collective reflection as people learn from one another.

Reflective conversations facilitate unfolding tacit knowledge as people share experiences, compare perceptions, and remember successes and failures. Tacit knowledge comes through experience and is difficult to articulate and teach to others. Yet when people share stories about experiences, their tacit knowing is tapped. As this knowledge becomes part of the group conversation, the organization is more able to retain the knowledge over time. A blend of individual and collective reflection provides experiential complements to training as well as a relatively inexpensive source of organizational learning. Designating for and allowing time for individual and collective reflection is an essential aspect of creating organization-wide enabling conditions.

My third and fourth complements to Nonaka's enabling conditions to improve the climate for knowledge creation involve the complementary and interdependent nature of *norms* and *boundaries* that define the space. Who is included and who is not? How do you know? Who decides? Norms and boundaries are invaluable clues to reading the organizational environment.

Group and organizational norms typically emerge and continue in profoundly unconscious ways. To become more conscious of the norms of a group that is important to you, think about what the group encourages you to do and discourages you from doing. For example, how do you know how to behave in the group? Who decides? How do you know if you belong in a group? Can people easily become a part of the group? How do you know who makes decisions? Your answers to these kinds of questions reveal part of the norms and boundary parameters of the group.

Embedded within norms are unexamined assumptions that create inertia. The less aware people are of what they are encouraged to do or discouraged from doing, the more the group's norms and boundaries shape their individual behaviors. As people notice and become aware of norms and patterns, they can consciously decide whether to continue the pattern or to alter behavior. The more unconscious the norms and the more rigid the boundaries, the less adaptive the prevailing behavior is.

Impervious boundaries segregate groups of people. They can keep out people who seem different even when they might be invaluable resources for the group. Norms that sustain the status quo close out diverse perspectives, even among the people who are already a part of the group. For example, a common pattern is for a group to listen to certain members more than others, thus giving those few people more influence. One way the pattern remains unchanged is to have norms that explicitly discourage

Figure 6.3   **Enabling conditions for the quality of the conversational space**

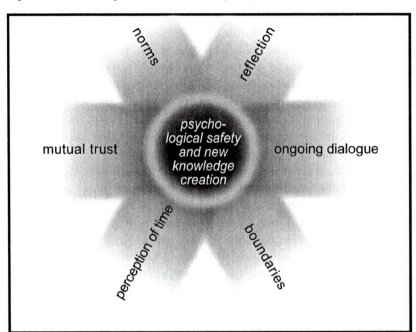

and minimize the influence of specific group members by interrupting them when they speak or by ignoring their input. As elaborated in Chapter 4, when group members perpetuate these patterns unconsciously, these silenced people have less leverage for influence and change. With more awareness and recognition of the patterns, participants can choose whether or not they want to continue the patterns (see Figure 6.3).

To summarize, the quality of the conversational space depends upon mutual trust that supports ongoing dialogue, reflection that requires time, and consciousness that alters norms and boundaries. These six enabling conditions are guiding principles for organizations to intentionally improve their communication and innovation through the creation of new knowledge.

Nature of Energy in the Space

Conversational spaces also have a tone or a feeling. In some, the energy can be described as an urgency that *pushes* people, such as pushing for results, decisions, or agreement. In others, the energy attracts, or *pulls,* people toward behaviors, such as toward inquiry or reflection. Pushing and pulling energies feel different and have markedly dissimilar impacts on the context (see Figure 6.4). Each approach is preferable in some situations and less effective in others. An organizational challenge exists in how to make these distinctions proactively instead of going along blindly or assuming that "one size fits all." The challenge is in learning how to use combinations of these approaches to serve the long-term interests of the organization and its varied stakeholders.

Pushing is especially useful when the group must accomplish prompt results. Pushing is critical in emergencies. On the other hand, controversial, complex situations necessitate drawing upon, or pulling for, diverse and sometimes subtle perspectives. Participants need to bring their differences to the surface in conversations of inquiry and catalytic conversations to expose each other to new information, contrary perspectives, and a wider range of possibilities. Using a conversational learning approach involves pulling for reflection and inquiry. It is enhanced when people can temporarily suspend judgment long enough to explore a range of perspectives, construct new meanings, and transform collective experiences (Baker et al. 2002). Then, at some point, the pushing energy prompts closure and forward movement.

Where results and outcomes are the singular priority, often the approaches used to gain the results depend on streamlined linear thinking that I refer to as *sparse linearity.* When this streamlined approach is used, people spend less time and energy on brainstorming than on dividing responsibilities. They spend less time and energy on seeking diverse perspectives than on eliciting directly relevant input. They spend less time and energy on exploring the root causes of controversies than on addressing the steps required to meet a deadline.

The sparseness, ideal for efficiency in the short run, leaves groups and organizations vulnerable when they face highly complex situations or intensely controversial issues. For example, when a pharmaceutical company faces undue pressure to get a new medication to market, a sparsely linear approach may leave it especially vulnerable to product recalls and increased legal action. Silencing opponents to a land development project may result in an expedited permit approval in the short run but may ultimately lead to extended delays due to litigation and court appeals from angry stakeholders.

The distinction between sparse linearity and pulling for inquiry is

Figure 6.4 **Different energies in the conversational space**

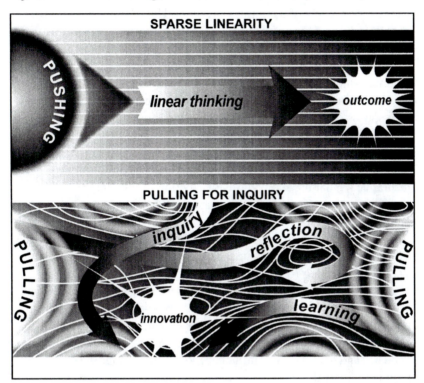

analogous to what is commonly referred to in the organizational learning and knowledge management literature as the differences among single-loop, double-loop, and triple-loop learning (Argyris 1994, 1997; Isaacs 1993; Romme and van Witteloostuijn 1999). When an organization faces a challenge, often responses address the symptoms of the problem without delving beneath the surface to understand more about the underlying causes. This mode entails single-loop learning and is analogous to sparse linearity. Alternatively, as organizations examine root causes of issues and underlying norms, they engage in double-loop learning. Triple-loop learning is rare because it requires the organization to explore underlying assumptions and to question the most fundamental processes.

To illustrate these three approaches, let's think about health care and the growing number of the uninsured in the United States. The Consolidated Omnibus Budget Reconciliation Act (COBRA), passed in

1986, created a program that reflects a single-loop learning approach to address symptoms of a complex problem. Under this program, when a person leaves a job, he or she can continue the same health insurance by assuming the cost of the individual premium for about 18 months. COBRA offers a valuable bridge for people who have short periods of unemployment between jobs and who can afford to pay the premiums.

A double-loop learning approach involves gathering data to identify root causes of problems. In this case, it would require consideration of health care costs, the current insurance system, and system-wide normative patterns beneath the surface. For example, what are the sources of health insurance? Who pays for it? Who has and does not have health insurance? What are the patterns of coverage? What care is and is not available without insurance? Who pays for that care? What is the impact on health care costs? What are the economic and employment impacts? An analysis of underlying patterns, norms, and complexities is critical as distinct from addressing surface symptoms in single-loop learning. Therefore, pushing for quick results is not adequate.

A triple-loop learning approach requires an even more fundamental reframing of the issue as well as who is involved in making decisions. For example, who participates in decision making about health care quality, costs, and insurance coverage? Who is heard and who is not heard? Who has and does not have influence? What are the long-term economic implications of the answers to these questions? Where are the hidden costs of health care? What are the societal and human implications? The approach involves an examination of root causes of the situation, the overlapping decision-making processes, and the long-term costs to individuals, businesses, and the government.

Thus, in the triple-loop example, the changes extend beyond health care insurance and costs to the whole *process* and its *participants*. A triple-loop process dramatically changes the *degree* to which there is exploration of the complex root causes and who is involved in the decision making. People likely affected by changes to the status quo would have input and influence and in some way be included in the decision making. People with differing perspectives and dissimilar needs would be actively involved, and their information and input would be part of the data collected.

Most organizational issues rarely call for the elaborate triple-loop process. Working constructively through multiple, interlocking dimensions of issues is a convoluted process. Working constructively through differences of perspective among diverse stakeholders is time-consuming. Yet organizations often face complex issues that require the more elaborate processes and deeper kinds of conversation involved in double-loop thinking. When organizations only address the symptoms of major challenges, the problems do not go away. Instead, they fester and increase over time.

By exploring the implications of using these three approaches, it is easier to see how sparse processes and complex approaches vis-à-vis organizational communication are oxymorons. Sparse linearity cannot accommodate conflicting perspectives, in-depth research, or overlapping contexts. Sparse linearity also does not lend itself to breaking out of the status quo, a process that more often than not depends on diverse perspectives to spark catalytic conversations and innovative approaches. Rycroft and Kash's (1999) research demonstrates that complex networks and knowledge organizations cannot be forced, or pushed, into innovation. Instead, their research shows that organizations must create contexts that support (pull for) innovation much as Nonaka's (1994) organization-wide enabling conditions do.

Benefits of Attending to the Space

As mentioned earlier, Nonaka and many other experts in knowledge management and organizational learning recognize the interdependencies that exist among individual and collective learning. For Nonaka (1994), while "ideas are formed in the minds of individuals, interaction between individuals typically plays a critical role in developing these ideas . . . 'communities of interaction' contribute to the amplification and development of new knowledge" (p. 15). Brown and Duguid (1991, 2000) and Wenger (1998) explore these groups as communities of practice that promote learning and new knowledge creation. They highlight the interdependency between *organizational conversations* that promote learning and the *environments* in which they occur. Conversational contexts that amplify and develop learning and new knowledge creation are scenarios in which people listen to and learn from each other's differences. These spaces have boundaries fluid enough for self-organizing communities of practice to emerge as is encouraged by the organizational learning and knowledge management literature (Argyris 1997; Bohm 1996; Brown and Duguid 1991, 2000; Lave and Wenger 1991; Nonaka 1994; Schrage 1990; Wenger 1998).

In organizational life, people also make sense of what is going on around them within overlapping networks of individual, group, organizational, and societal contexts. The nature of these contexts and spaces influence whether reflection, catalytic conversations, conversational learning, and other kinds of constructive conversations occur. Communities of practice are more likely to spontaneously surface when the structure and tenor of the context does not impede them. Learning and innovation are more likely to emerge in receptive spaces where people can openly talk about possibilities and differences. However, organizations must intentionally create the enabling conditions for conversational spaces that support inquiry, temporary suspension of judgment, reflection, and innovation.

One way to realize the benefits of receptive conversational space in organizations is by recognizing the increased leverage that quality space brings to people and to organizations. *Quality* and *leverage* function in concert with each other as mirror images. They represent inseparable facets of congruity and long-term well-being of organizations. Whether working in or among organizations or preparing people to do this work, the potential leverage of anticipating how to create high quality, supportive work environments can hardly be overestimated.

This type of leverage is distinctly different from covert manipulation, which is more contradictory than congruent. Trying to use space as a technique to manipulate people reveals incongruity and only increases apathy and cynicism rather than helping diverse stakeholders accomplish lasting, constructive change. Like other sources of power, fostering the space entails the responsibility to use it wisely. When trust, psychological safety, reflection, permeable boundaries, and inclusive norms characterize the quality of the space, it provides a foundation for constructive interactions that support superordinate goals that extend beyond immediate self-interest. Rather than behaving reactively, people can be more proactive in anticipating changes and issues. The likelihood of recognizing opportunities in a changing world is increased because of the rich collective knowledge available. Impending changes can surface through collective reflection that taps the tacit and explicit ways of seeing, knowing, and working in the world more than when isolated task completion is the primary modus operandi. Asking questions, acknowledging shortcomings, requesting help, sharing ideas, and exchanging information give rise to relationship building and innovative brainstorming.

It is a challenge to create environments that invite constructive interactions. Learning how to work effectively with diverse people, bring up volatile issues productively, disagree usefully, talk about divergent opinions, and challenge the assumed norms are all hard work. These behaviors require considerable effort, skill building, and conducive spaces that support catalytic conversations as part of the ongoing organizational practices.

Complementary Conversational Mediums

Organizations face major communication challenges as they try to bring diverse, interdependent stakeholders into alignment to work together toward a collective vision and alternative future (Kotter 1996). Traditionally, conversations were primarily face-to-face experiences in concrete, physical environments. Organizations must now support diverse complementary environments and as many mediums for expression as possible. Conversational spaces need to accommodate a wide range of interactional formations and sizes within and among organizations: pairs of people, groups, subgroups, interorganizational groups, and large groups. These spaces need to accommodate people who have vastly different communication styles and preferences with appropriate contexts (formal or informal, routine or ad hoc, planned or self-organized.

In the same way that some people prefer one-on-one interactions while others thrive in large groups, it is important for organizations to offer complementary and diverse environments for communication. They must provide a variety of actual and virtual conversational spaces and project venues and ensure that people have ample opportunities to easily access and use all of them as needed. These approaches invite more people into conversation, while offering everyone at least one medium that feels engaging and comfortable enough to encourage more participation. Chapter 7 elaborates on these ideas.

Notes

1. For conciseness in this chapter, I most often will use the word *space* though often these other words can be substituted.

2. My use of the word *social,* as in social interactions or social life, does not refer to leisurely activities. Instead, *social* refers to interpersonal dynamics in group, organizational, and interorganizational settings.

References

Argyris, C. 1994. Good communication that blocks learning. *Harvard Business Review* (July): 77–85.

———. 1997. *On organizational learning.* Oxford, UK: Blackwell Business.

Baker, A. C. 1995. Bridging differences and learning through conversation. Published dissertation. http://www.ohiolink.edu/etd/view.cgi?acc_num=case1058882651.

Baker, A. C., P. J. Jensen, and D. A. Kolb. 2002. *Conversational learning: An experiential approach to knowledge creation.* Westport, CT: Quorum Books.

———. 2005. Conversation as experiential learning. *Management Learning: The Journal for Managerial and Organizational Learning* 36 (4): 411–427.

Block, P. 2000. *Flawless consulting: A guide to getting your expertise used.* 2nd Edition. San Francisco: Jossey-Bass.

Bohm, D. 1996. *On dialogue,* ed. L. Nichol. New York: Routledge.

Brown, J. S., and P. Duguid. 1991. Organizational learning and communities-of-practice: Toward a unified view of working, learning and innovation. *Organization Science* 2 (1): 40–57.

———. 2000. *The social life of organization.* Boston: Harvard Business School Press.

Dess, Gregory G., and Joseph C. Picken. 2000. Changing role: Leadership in the 21st Century. *Organizational Dynamics* 28 (3): 18–34.

Edmondson, A. 1996. Learning from mistakes is easier said than done: Group and organizational influences on the detection and correction of human error. *Journal of Applied Behavioral Science* 32: 5–28.

———. 1999. Psychological safety and learning behavior. *Administrative Science Quarterly* 44: 350–383.

Hall, E. T. 1966. *The hidden dimension.* Garden City, NY: Doubleday.

Isaacs, W. 1993. Taking flight: Dialogue, collective thinking, and organizational learning. *Organizational Dynamics* 22 (2): 24–39.

Isaacs, W. 1999. Dialogue and the art of thinking together. New York: Currency.

Jacobs, C. D., and L. T. Heracleous. 2005. Answers for questions to come: Reflective dialogue as an enabler of strategic innovation. *Journal of Organizational Change Management* 18 (4): 338–352.

Kotter, J. P. 1996. *Leading change.* Boston, MA: Harvard Business School Press.

Lave, J., and E. Wenger. 1991. *Situated learning: Legitimate peripheral participation.* New York: Cambridge University Press.

Nonaka, I. 1994. A dynamic theory of organizational knowledge creation. *Organization Science* 5 (1): 14–37.

Romme, G. L., and A. van Witteloostruijn. 1999. Circular organizing and triple loop learning. *Journal of Organizational Change Management* 12 (5): 439–453.

Rycroft, R. W., and D. E. Kash. 1999. *The complexity challenge: Technological innovation for the 21st Century.* New York: Pinter.

Schein, E. H. 2004. *Organizational culture and leadership.* San Francisco, CA: John Wiley & Sons, Inc.

Schon, D. 1983. The structure of reflection-in-action. In *The reflective practitioner: How professionals think in action,* 128–167. New York: Basic Books.

Schrage, M. 1990. *Shared minds: The new technologies of collaboration.* New York: Random House.

Von Krogh, G., K. Ichijo, and I. Nonaka. 2000. *Enabling knowledge creation: How to unlock the mystery of tacit knowledge and release the power of innovation.* Oxford, UK: Oxford University Press.

Wenger, E. 1998. *Communities of practice: Learning, meaning, and identity.* New York: Cambridge University Press.

Winnicott, D. W. 1992. *Psycho-analytic explorations.* Cambridge, MA: Harvard University Press.

Wyss-Flamm, E. D. 2003. Conversational learning in teams: A dynamic model for individual and group development. Paper presented at the annual meeting of the Academy of Management, Seattle, WA.

Wyss-Flamm, E. D. 2003. Exploring democratic process in multicultural teams: A conversation-centered research approach. Paper presented at the annual meeting of the Academy of Management, Seattle, WA.

7

Complementary Technologies for Catalytic Conversations

Computers, electronics, hardware, software—these are images commonly associated with the word *technology,* yet technologies have long been a part of people's lives. Technologies are the mediums through which people alter their environment or produce things. The ancient Romans, for example, built aqueducts to move water long distances.

Technologies as Social Phenomena

Technologies shape a society's culture and environment while at the same time a society's culture shapes technologies. Highways enable people to travel and move goods long distances with relative ease and speed. Highways contribute to the mobility of the population and profoundly influence land use, as housing and commercial centers develop in close proximity to good roads. At the same time, the physical environment affects the placement and cost of roads; politics affect funding, location, and regulatory decisions; and economics affect the demand for and funding of highways.

During the last half of the twentieth century in the United States, transportation patterns and taxation policies dramatically altered land development patterns, leading to what is now referred to as *sprawl,* by enabling people to live greater distances from city centers. Technological advances and a booming economy made it easier and more cost-effective to build superhighways, bridges, and tunnels and for people to buy vehicles that could travel at faster speeds. Many people lament the sprawl, long commutes, increasing gas prices, and lack of community, but daily life in many areas of the United States depends heavily on access to cars for transportation. The interdependency of technologies and political, economic, physical, and cultural environments led to these patterns. Likewise, changing those patterns will require fundamental alterations on multiple fronts.

"Because they are the products of human choice and design, technologies embody social, cultural, and political values, and are inherently social phenomena. Thus, instead of focusing only on '*what* is technology,' we need to ask '*who* is technology?'" (La Porte 2002, 1) We depend on energy resources to supply electricity, heat homes and offices, and power cars. The technologies that provide this energy (the concrete "whats")— refineries, coal mines, solar panels, river dams, transmission lines, wind farms, and nuclear power plants—have environmental impact and present advantages and challenges to engineering, science, and cost.

The "whos" are the people and groups that influence and make decisions along the energy demand-and-supply chain. It is important to understand the "whos" within a political milieu and in relation to particular cultural values and market forces. These "whos" individually and collectively influence choices about energy demand, use, and sources. The social aspects of technology come to life as people communicate with one another and juggle conflicting pressures.

The mediums through which people communicate, work, negotiate, and make sense of alternatives are also forms of technology [e.g., telephones, face-to-face (f2f) meetings, e-mails, letters, and faxes]. These mediums each enhance, serve, or inhibit preferred kinds of communication. To reiterate, a primary purpose of this book is to encourage quality conversations that support generative change and new knowledge creation. This chapter focuses on the selection of communication technologies that are most appropriate to realize those goals.

Complementary Technologies

Wise decisions about changing technologies grow out of considerations for the nature of work, the context, the impacts, access issues, and time frame, as well as what is comfortable and uncomfortable and for whom. For instance, do communication mediums encourage collaborative interaction, or do they inundate recipients with information and demands to address short-term goals? Do people need to meet f2f or do they have f2f meetings because that is how it has always been done? Does the technology increase access to relevant information and influence for everyone or only for a specific group? Does it promote reactive behavior, proactive behavior, or a combination?

These decisions need to grow out of the whats, whos, and whys of technology and consideration of short- and long-term implications. By questioning the common, and often unconscious, assumptions about ideal ways to communicate, people can collectively discover unexpected combinations of technologies that are complementary toward each other. *Complementary*[1] is the operative word in this chapter.

Whether varied approaches are complementary depends partially on the purpose of the work. If simple transmission of information and uni-directional communication is the only requirement, a relatively simple technology such as e-mail may be adequate. However, for the vast number of knowledge organizations and knowledge workers engaged in complex processes, these simple communication modes are woe-fully inadequate because continuous improvement and new knowledge creation are necessary.

This is especially true when complex situations require higher order thinking and innovation, "the social context or community which is created during the learning process has a major impact on the form and nature of the learning activities, the quality of dialogue, and the learn-ing outcomes" (McLoughlin 1999, 240). Experience is always situated within a specific context (Lave and Wenger 1991). Thus, the complex, knowledge-intensive organizational context requires communication modalities that facilitate the desirable behavior. The design must be intentional and proactive.

Complementary technologies that give people choices and influence can improve communication, learning, and adaptability. However, deciding between the everchanging, vast array of new technologies is complicated. Organizations must offer diverse combinations of tech-nologies to give people a wide range of possibilities. At the same time, adopting the newest technological fad can be inefficient, unproductive, and dangerous, and may bring unexpected consequences.

To discern whether a combination of modalities is complementary, it is necessary to ask a variety of questions. What is the purpose of the communication? What is the nature of the conversation's content? Who will be influenced? Who will be affected by decisions? Are they included? What are the expectations? Are participants willing? Do people have easy access to a choice of complementary technologies? Are the participants prepared to engage in combined technologies?

Choice of Technologies

One of the most useful and challenging combinations of communication technologies to foster change and innovation is to blend *f2f* and *virtual*[2] technologies. Increasingly, the geographic dispersion of people who work and play together, frequent travel needs, different time zones, congested metropolitan traffic, and differing internal body clocks among those who are morning people and those who are night owls limit the viability of depending solely on f2f interactions.

One such obstacle is the tendency of some people to communicate in habitual ways—e.g., in person, on line, in writing. They may choose one over the other because they have more experience, expertise, or comfort in one arena than another. For instance, an individual or group with strong technical skills and interests or who grew up using technology is much more accustomed to virtual communication and may not enjoy or have particularly well-developed people skills, and vice versa. However, regardless of habits, the complementary use of multiple mediums usually is necessary and fruitful. By using multiple mediums, people have alternatives and choices that better accommodate their differences in communication style, culture, and language of origin.

The manager of one global team indicated that sometimes "international partners are not comfortable with English . . . on a conference call" and that "accents can be tricky." This team "found that people could type English better than they could speak it. [Writing] made everything so much smoother" (Overholt 2002, 3). Even among all native speakers of language, some people will be more able to express themselves in writing. On the other hand, others are more comfortable with talking than they are with written communication. By providing a variety of mediums for participation, each individual is more likely to find at least one medium in which they thrive. As a result, organizations access a wider range of talent and expertise from among their employees and stakeholders.

Besides expertise and comfort levels, expectations influence communication habits. People's prior relationships and experiences influence their expectations. When participants have apprehensions or reservations about using technology or about the people with whom they will be working, virtual communication can actually "amplify the cultural dimensions of communication, task analysis, and problem-solving" (Newman, Griffen, and Cole 1989). When there are differences in experience or culture, the technology may actually accentuate the differences rather than minimize them because of the lack of visual cues and other limitations of specific technologies.

People's expectations about authority and decision making often influence their expectations regarding communication. A person from a high-power distant culture (Hofstede, 1997) or highly hierarchical culture typically does not expect, for example, to have direct contact with decision makers. Someone from this type of culture expects more distance to exist between those who hold the power and those in less powerful positions. Thus, this person may not expect to have much influence on decision makers and may be more willing to go along with decisions made from above. When people from diverse backgrounds are working together on a project team, they naturally bring these expectations into the online environment too, often presenting a new array of challenges. One's socialization regarding relationships to and distance from powerful decision makers will commonly influence expectations about whether it is appropriate to contact leaders directly or to ask for changes in procedures.

A third variable on habitual patterns is whether people tailor their mode of communication to the purpose of the interaction. One major distinction, as mentioned earlier, is whether the purpose is the linear *transmission* of existing information, *sharing* of information and knowledge, or *creating* new knowledge. This variable is one of the most challenging when communication patterns are habitual, because it requires openness to adaptation and the skill to differentiate the purpose and select the most appropriate medium accordingly. Changing the habit requires flexibility, judgment, and competence in other modes of communication.

Even more challenging is when the purpose of the communication is multifaceted, such as when sharing is a necessary precursor to the need for creating new knowledge toward becoming more innovative. If the purpose of the interaction is solely to transmit information, a person may be accustomed to a linear, unidirectional communication, such as a f2f monologue in which questions are discouraged or impossible. If a habitual mode of communication is unidirectional, one challenge is competence with other modes. A second challenge is knowing when and whether to step back and ask if that mode stymies the current situation and potential opportunity. Unidirectional communication that limits input and interaction can lead to incomplete information, misunderstanding, and information hoarding. It certainly thwarts complex learning, creativity, and innovation.

If the situation requires knowledge sharing and creating, interactive mediums are more appropriate. The organization needs a "building process of shared information [that] works like the coral reef, built in a fractal formation . . . as opposed to a linear mode" (Davis and Brewer 1997, 137). Complementary technologies provide ideal mediums for participants to build virtual "coral reefs." However, the organization must intentionally select, provide, and support a combination of technologies that promote fluid, open sharing of information, exploration of possibilities, and creation of new knowledge. The complementary technologies can help stakeholders build a context that promotes interactive give and take, conversational learning, and catalytic conversations to promote innovation.

Knowledge sharing and creativity grow out of social, relational dynamics. "Knowledge is not just embedded in the invisible cognitive worlds of individuals, but exists within the multiple relationships and evolving memberships of individuals and groups in society" (Richter 1998, 312). Rigid structures, competitive conduct, and excessive rationality impede them. Organizations must create conditions that serve the needs of diverse people, types of work, specific contexts, and overarching aims. They can specifically design and use technologies that facilitate cognitive learning and the development of *multiple relationships and evolving memberships of individuals and groups* to promote a culture of fluid knowledge sharing and creativity. Diverse people participating in fluid conversations can minimize polarization and increase creativity as people share across diverse communities. Although complementary technologies can support the transmission of information, the focus here is to support the more complex demands for proactive problem solving, creativity, and innovation.

Thus, organizations can anticipate the influences that reinforce people to continue to use habitual communication patterns; that is, deferring to comfort level, expectations, or assumed purpose. Although context is a part of conversation in any venue, in the virtual world anticipating and planning the context is even more critical. The design of the virtual environment, the nature of the content, the charge given to participants, prior relationships, and cultural differences are all variables that need to be anticipated and considered to maximize the likelihood that the virtual components will support, rather than distract from, the quality of the interactions and, thus, the work. Decisions about how one medium complements another should be based upon these kinds of considerations.

Blended Learning as Distinct from
Complementary Technologies

Blended learning is increasingly popular in organizational online settings. The term *blended learning* is a current catchphrase for combining "virtual and physical learning experiences" (Overholt 2002, 2). The range of possibilities available for virtual communication is changing so rapidly that any list becomes quickly outdated. In addition to the Internet and e-mail, examples of virtual technologies include intranets, extranets, groupware technologies, Internet-based virtual meeting platforms, webinars, wikis, Web-conferencing software, videoconferencing, electronic document–based systems, computer simulations, instructor-led training (ILT), facilities-based learning/training, self-paced e-learning content development tools, offline learning materials (CD-ROMs and iPods), job aids, labs, mentoring (ways to get questions answered and problems solved immediately and without f2f contact), mentoring/instructor-led support, discussion boards/chat rooms, online instruction, text and electronic media, scenario-based exercises (SBEs), assessments, frequently asked questions (FAQs) resources, and full-featured software tied to actual use by and feedback to the learner.

On the surface, it may seem as if blended learning and complementary technologies are the same, and they do share many important characteristics. There are, however, distinct differences. Blended learning is generally related to employee training programs. According to the International Data Corporation (IDC), an organization integrally involved in blended learning uses "any possible combination of a wide range of learning delivery media designed to solve specific business problems" (Brennan 2003).

Complementary technology as described here is broader and may or may not directly relate to training, education, or solving specific problems. The emphasis is on expanding the nature and variety of communication mediums to more effectively meet organizational needs for more innovation, flexibility, and creativity. Designers of complementary technologies intentionally anticipate how to meet the preferences, access the expertise, and generate interactions among diverse stakeholders. The approach must tap a wide spectrum of human interactions that make up actual everyday organizational practices and collaboration among people to enable them to be more creative and innovative than they otherwise could be without the cross-fertilization. The key distinction between blended learning and complementary technologies is between simply transmitting information or the complex processes of sharing and creating new knowledge.

Online Communication

Using complementary technologies is especially timely and critical because of the complex challenges faced by organizations. The theoretical and practical literature is increasingly filled with studies that demonstrate the inseparability of the quality of relationships, the quality of organizational communication, and an organization's capacity to create new knowledge (Agarwal 2003; Griffith, Sawyer, and Neale 2003; Scott 2000; Weedman 1999). The caveat is that bringing these assets together in ingenious ways demands managerial approaches that are quite different from traditional managerial models.

In a study of a global high-tech firm, Scott found that "the most significant barrier to virtual relationships and learning in collaborations is lack of trust . . ." (Scott 2000, 84). Mutual trust is critical for the rapid, collaborative, transnational development of global high-tech firm's products. The virtual integration of members of the firm, customers, suppliers, and other external stakeholders through interorganizational learning was essential to increase the firm's capability to draw upon widely dispersed talent and their capacity for fast response across distance and time zones.

The more people in the firm needed to challenge fundamental assumptions, learn new skills, and create new knowledge, the more critical trusting relationships were among the participants (Scott 2000). Therefore, in virtual environments, as people work more interdependently trust becomes a more significant issue.

> If parties do not trust each other, dialogue may prove itself as rather naïve and unrealistic. There will always be the chance that one of the parties, probably the most powerful one, takes advantage of the situation and imposes itself on the other parties . . . [W]hat is needed . . . is establishing trust. (van der Smagt 2000, 152)

There are two indispensable considerations for designing complementary technologies: ample opportunity for participant interaction and support for the development of relationships of trust, psychological safety, and mutual accountability. To be fully complementary, organizations must invest in relationship building as well as in technology. These approaches foster the capacity of individuals to continuously learn, to adapt to changes, to be proactive, and to be innovative (Edmondson 1999, 2003; Rycroft and Kash 1999; Scott 2000).

Online conversation environments provide unbounded space to expand this kind of interaction (Forrester 1991; Griffith et al. 2003). Unlike f2f conversations, asynchronous conversations allow participants to read comments when convenient, to reread them at will, and to choose when or whether to respond. The online, reflective conversation can lend itself to creating "knowledge that is deeper rooted and more flexible than knowledge obtained otherwise" (Holsbrink-Engels 1997, 429). Well-designed and facilitated spaces play a unique role in expanding access and promoting reflection. For instance, in my research with an online community, there was an ongoing conversation about a controversial topic. After reading a quite direct question, a recipient responded,

> I am going to answer your question. However, it is late tonight, and I want to give some time to my answer and not just fire off a quick response. So I'm going to mull this over tomorrow and try to paint a picture of who I am and how my beliefs . . . were formed.

The next day, he did write a thoughtful and open response that contributed to the further deepening of the conversation that continued for several weeks within the group. Thus, another significant advantage to the virtual world is that it allows for a kind of behind-the-scenes reflection and reconsideration of prejudgments or prejudices (Gadamer 1994; Kimball and Garrison 1999).

Online conversations about controversial topics encourage more reflection for some people than do f2f venues. When f2f, many people feel more compelled to respond immediately to comments. The response might be conveyed verbally, through body language and expressions, or by exiting from the situation. At times, these immediate responses are more reactive than responsive or reflective. A unique distinction between f2f and online conversational environments is that in the latter, each person reads as an individual. People can choose to respond right away or to use private time and space to reflect before answering. They may take days or weeks to respond, or simply choose not to respond. This privacy and added reflection at times enable people to listen and understand others' experiences, stories, and ideas at their own pace and in new ways without the immediate f2f pressure of responding in the moment.

Undoubtedly this arena is one that helps some people to be expressive, have thoughtful reflections, and increase collaborative understanding. On the other hand, many others may choose to be only "readers" and not engage actively in the conversation by posting comments. Still others may choose to stop reading and may quietly or openly opt out of the conversation altogether.

Regardless, when used carefully and responsibly, online environments can provide another medium for talking about important and delicate issues by accommodating differences among diverse people. They provide another venue for catalytic conversation and proactive intervention for regenerative change in organizations. By returning again and again to conversations about valued work, people in interdependent relationships can continuously reshape their understandings and consequently foster adaptability in organizations. Expanding access to informal, exploratory conversations serves the organization and its people.

Moving Forward Using Complementary Technologies

In spite of the benefits, many are skeptical about online conversations. I can speak from personal experience as someone who, until about thirteen years ago, had previously relied on f2f interactions as the ideal medium for my work as a manager, professor, and organizational culture and change consultant. As a nontechnical person, I was skeptical about using online conversational environments, especially when I worked with people who had divergent values, assumptions, and experiences and who needed to work on issues that were rife with tension. My perspective changed as I used, observed, participated, and researched multiple online conversational environments. Even for difficult conversations, virtual environments and f2f venues can be complementary, appropriate, and rewarding.

Groupware technologies, such as Microsoft SharePoint and IBM's Lotus QuickPlace and Quickr, support these online conversational spaces. In addition to conversation spaces, groupware technologies usually support a variety of other virtual interactions to facilitate collaboration among people who are geographically and temporally dispersed. For example, Internet-based virtual meeting platforms, Web-conferencing software, and videoconferencing provide different forums for colleagues to see each other as they work together when they are not physically in the same place. Electronic document-based systems make it easier for people to create jointly written documents without the limitations of same time–same space barriers and without having to leave their own personal computers.

The importance of anticipating issues related to software and hardware are paramount. Does everyone have speedy, reliable access from wherever they may need it? Is the software easy to use? Do people know how to use it before they begin? Does everyone have compatible software and hardware? Is it flexible enough to provide a variety of ways for people to participate, such as importing documents, initiating topics, adding threads and rooms, and creating links? Is it flexible enough to support creativity and innovation? Is there easy 24/7 (or as much as possible) access to technical help and support? Are there incentives for people to want to participate? Frequently these issues are not anticipated, which can seriously damage a project and diminish participation and learning. Preventing problems is far more efficient than correcting them later.

When people hear the term *online conversational spaces,* they frequently think about chat rooms and blogs, partially because they are so common and readily available on the Internet. The conversational spaces on which I am focusing are dramatically different and are a much more deliberate kind of environment that is useful in many ways. In human terms, online conversational spaces provide valuable benefits. In economic terms, they can provide a good return on the initial investment.

Online conversational spaces offer opportunities for interaction that are also distinctly different from e-mail conversations. E-mail is ideal for the efficient linear transmission of information and for coordinating activities. Likewise, it is one essential way to share existing information and thus not continuously "reinvent the wheel." Online conversational spaces, on the other hand, provide opportunities that are more conducive to sharing diverse perspectives, exploring new possibilities, discovering novel ideas, and creating broader understanding. They function much like gatherings around a conference table or a dining room table, in a seminar room or a living room, or other similar f2f gatherings. These virtual environments may look and work much like rooms where people have virtual meetings, exploratory conversations, and brainstorming sessions. Access is limited to a mutually agreed-upon, predetermined group of participants. People cannot *drop in* unless invited and given access through user names and passwords.

Online conversations can be synchronistic, with participants all engaged in conversation at the same time, although rarely in the same place. Or they can be set up asynchronously, allowing participants to join the conversation at whatever time of the day or night is convenient for them and from almost anywhere in the world. Often the software makes it possible for groups to use both synchronous and asynchronous spaces. This virtual combination would be similar to a group having f2f meetings for part of its work and using virtual mediums, such as conference calls and e-mail, for other dimensions of the work.

Asynchronous online conversation spaces are typically divided into *rooms,* much as physical spaces are. Often there is an open space that functions much like a living room or conference room where everyone in the group can participant in the conversation. There are also rooms for conversations on specific topics. At any one time, there are multiple conversations taking place on varied topics. Each conversation is separated into a different thread or folder, organized by topic. In this virtual configuration, people can usually contribute to as many or as few of the threaded (topical) conversations as they wish, initiate new threads (topics), post and share resources in the archives or library folder, and create links for one another to supplementary resources. There can be additional rooms created for subgroups or smaller project teams with either open access or access restricted to team members.

Unlike f2f and most synchronous conversations, the time and space available for asynchronous participation is essentially unlimited. If you forgot to say something in a previous f2f or online conversation or as you think of new things you want to say or questions to ask, you can spontaneously *talk* by posting additional comments. This option offers enormous flexibility. Other participants will find your contributions when they sign on, or you can alert them to your new entry via an e-mail or text message.

Groups and organizations can tailor the combination of technologies to the nature of their work, expectations, intentions, availability of resources, and so on. However, to facilitate the added values of *sharing* and *creating* knowledge, it is critical to intersperse complementary asynchronous online conversation spaces with intermittent f2f conversations (Baker 2002; Bal and Teo 2006; Horowitz, Bravington, and Silvis 2006; Pauleen and Yoong 2001). "[E]arly in the relationship face-to-face communication is ideal to establish trust and prevent misunderstanding . . . [it] reinforces strong ties by building affective trust" (Scott 2000, 105–106).

For instance, if a new project team is composed of people who live in different parts of the country or the world, they need to either begin their work together with several days of f2f meetings or have f2f time early in their work. The bulk of their project work can then be accomplished through groupware technologies to support their needs, interspersed with periodic f2f contact to revitalize and renew the relationships and to facilitate aspects of their work that are not conducive to the virtual sphere. A wide variety of additional virtual technologies and f2f mediums can be added as needed to further support the work.

Obviously, these online conversational spaces traverse boundaries of time and geography. Less obviously though, they open many other new streams of opportunities. People using the online spaces often find that they facilitate brainstorming and the spontaneous feeding off of each other's ideas. Some people also find it is easier to confront difficult issues and disagreements on line than it is in person. Yet, in the same way that most participants in catalytic conversations and conversational learning need to improve their capacity to engage in substantive f2f conversations, they also need to learn how to talk to each other in virtual environments in ways that effectively support the work.

Online conversations require specific intentional effort because visual cues are usually limited to written text, imported graphics, and audio cues. Virtual groups need to develop communication etiquette and take care to express thoughts clearly. It is especially important to develop social cues (how to smile, interrupt, yawn) and to explicitly let the readers know before changing subjects or shifting gears (Williams 1999). Avoiding anonymous postings increases personal responsibility for what people say and diminishes disparaging outbursts that damage relationships and impede learning.

As a group, participants need to create their own guidelines or norms for preferred behaviors. Each group and situation is somewhat unique, and what works in one place may not work in another. Counterintuitively, the more experience participants have, the more important it is not to skip this step, because previous experiences can lead to rigid expectations. It is unrealistic to expect participants to have the same expectations unless each new group spends at least a little time developing its own collective norms. By intentionally creating norms up front, the group can avoid sowing some of the seeds for conflict.

Here are some possible topics to consider as guidelines for online etiquette:

- The degree to which conversation will be free-flowing or structured
- The tone that the group hopes will characterize its work together (e.g., polite, direct)
- Directness or indirectness of language
- Perceptions about appropriate or inappropriate language
- Expectations about whether and how to give and receive feedback
- Confidentiality issues about sharing the conversations outside of the group
- Expectations about frequency of participation, volume of participation, length of posting
- How freely to introduce new issues and express disagreements
- Expectations about handling conflict

Norms give participants a touchstone, not a rigid prescription, for reference as the conversations evolve. They also provide a starting point from which to talk about needed changes.

Facilitators are another key component of the most successful and long-lasting online conversations. Facilitators with a light touch are optimum for online spaces designed to encourage shared creation, conversational learning, and catalytic conversations. By light touch, I mean the facilitator models ways to participate within the boundaries of the mutually created norms, rather than controlling the conversation in ways that impede potential creativity and enjoyment (Baker 2002; Williams 1999). The facilitator needs to encourage wide participation and to give the conversation just enough structure to keep it from meandering into nothingness, causing a loss of interest. A facilitator helps make up for the missing visual cues by alerting participants to next steps, such as who will take the lead on a project or topic or people who are not being heard and understood or are misunderstood.

In the online environment, the facilitator has even more responsibility than in f2f contexts to help participants anticipate how their language and behavior might be misunderstood. The facilitators may need to have occasional offline conversations with some participants to offer additional guidance. Often the role of facilitator rotates according to some framework, such as the nature of the current work, regular time intervals, or among participants with facilitator training. The rotation spreads out the investment and sense of responsibility for success while also developing facilitation skills throughout the organization.

No Ordinary Learning

Learning through complementary technologies can take on qualities that are quite different from memorization, transmission of factual information, or black-and-white thinking. In fact, thinking about ideas and possibilities in ways that demonstrate consideration of complex variables can be fostered by a combination of f2f and online contexts. They offer unique opportunities for writing, reading, reflecting, and speaking in ongoing conversations (Baker 2002; Forrester 1991; Gibbs 1999; Weedman 1999)

In the private sector, professional training and development and blended learning approaches as mentioned earlier seem to be most effective when they include opportunities for online interaction. Although the purpose of the training is more specific and contextually dependent and the online conversations are generally not as free-flowing, the most successful blended learning approaches include online opportunities for interaction (Thomson Job Impact Study 2002)[3]. Real-world learning in these training programs included online conversational interaction. For instance, online mentoring support includes spaces where learners and more seasoned employees could have online conversations, consider a variety of alternatives, ask questions, and share experiences.

Complex, intense conversations among people with differing interpretations are dynamic, nonlinear, ambiguous, and thus difficult to recall accurately. Verbal conversations cannot be recreated from memory, especially when they are fast-paced and about controversial topics. Online conversations are retrievable and allow the participants—and researchers—to read, reflect, and reread to continue learning. Some participants say that upon rereading, they realize that they often remembered part of the conversations inaccurately. Some say that revisiting online conversations after they end allows them to better understand comments made early in the conversation and helps develop deeper, subsequent f2f conversations. In the later reading, reflection and conversations, they have much more context, time, and opportunity for reflection. For example, in my research with an online community, one participant said,

> I have a feeling that I'm probably actually more authentic in online discussions than I am in face-to-face discussions because I'm not taking in . . . the body language, whatever is going on in the environment. You know, to me, it's hard to explain, but there's almost like a mental connection. To

borrow a term from [the name of another participant], the revisitability because you've got the other person's comments right there in front of you . . . I don't have to rely on my own memory.

This revisiting is another form of recursivity. It reinforces learning, allows participants to come back to ideas with the benefit of intervening experiences and reflections, and facilitates seeing things in new ways (Baker, Jensen, and Kolb 2002; Holsbrink-Engels 1997).

For example, in educational environments where courses are taught using a combination of f2f and online interactions, research with undergraduate and graduate students across disciplines suggests that learning can be expanded by participation in the online conversation. For example,

> Informal, exploratory, nonbinding conversation is essential to intellectual work. Research in the sciences, humanities, arts, and professions demonstrates that for many people, the opportunity to try out ideas among peers is central to . . . problem solving and developing new approaches. . . . [T]he most important learning students do happens outside the instructor's reach. (Weedman 1999, 920)

Online conversations in workplace and university settings can provide an unusual and fertile space for learning by combining the freedom for informal exploration with the awareness that there is some semblance of permanence to what they write and that peers and faculty will read the entries. These spaces encourage interactions that are far more substantive than chatting. The processes of writing down thoughts and ideas, reading and rereading one's own entries and those of others, bouncing ideas back and forth, refining and revising them with others, and hearing about the successes and shortcomings of others in online conversations, all contribute to new learning. By articulating thoughts, revising comments before posting an entry into the online space, and rereading the threads of conversation, learning is increased and deepened. Learning that is specifically related to work in organizational settings also benefits from online conversational spaces (Forrester 1991; Gibbs 1999; Weedman 1999).

Conclusions

Although the hardware and software of technology attract attention and have a jazzy appeal, the "true medium of collaboration is other people"

(Schrage 1989, 33). It is the *who* rather than the *what* of technology that makes things happen. The most challenging facets of the work involve facilitating constructive and innovative work among people.

Because human, interpersonal dynamics are so challenging, and unpredictable, it can be tempting to shift attention to things like computer hardware and software. These topics are more concrete, predictable, measurable, and controllable. The inescapable reality is that for technology to serve organizations beyond the simple transmission of information and to promote excellence and innovation, the participants and the quality of the conversations and relationships must be the primary resources and accordingly need to be the uppermost priorities.

Notes

1. I use the word *complementary* because it connotes more than simply supplementing, exchanging, or alternating. It signifies an active and intentional process that expands the potential of the communication for collaboration and innovation. It involves selecting a combination of mediums that build on one another. Because organizations and their stakeholders are interdependent, people must be able to constantly learn from each other and adapt for organizations to thrive in rapidly changing environments.

2. The word *virtual* describes mediums for communication and human interactions when people are not physically present in the same visual or audio field.

3. Thomson Job Impact Study, Phase I (2002), Phase II (2003), "200 employees at all organizational levels across a wide range of industries, including aerospace, computing, and manufacturing. The research was conducted in collaboration with Lockheed-Martin; NCR; Thomson Financial; Utah State University; University of Limerick, Ireland; Anoka-Ramsey Community College, Minnesota; and Executive Service Corps of Chicago" (2003 report, p. 2). The study compared five groups, one of which was a control group that received no training before attempting the real-world tasks. Three of the groups had some combination of blended learning opportunities, and one group "received a full NETg online course that included online mentoring, FAQs, Web sites, and books" (p. 3). The three blended groups had combinations, all of which included scenario-based exercises (SBEs) as the basis for learning software. "All three blended learning groups . . . performed nearly identically on the real-world tasks, ranging from 153 percent to 163 percent better accuracy than the control group (no training) and between 27 percent and 32 percent better accuracy than the e-Learning group.

References

Agarwal, R. 2003. Teamwork in the netcentric organization. In *International handbook of organizational teamwork and cooperative working,* ed. M. A. West, D. Tjosvold, and K. G. Smith, 443–462. West Sussex, UK: John Wiley & Sons Ltd.

Baker, A. C. 2002. Extending the conversation cyberspace. In *Conversational learning: An experiential approach to knowledge creation*, 165–183. Westport, CT: Quorum Books.

Baker, A. C., P. Jensen, and D. Kolb. 2002. *Conversational learning: An experiential approach to knowledge creation.* Westport, CT: Quorum Books.

Bal, J., and P. Teo. 2006. Implementing virtual teamworking: Part 2–A literature review. *Handbook of Business Strategy* 14 (3): 208–222.

Brennan, M. 2003. Blended learning and business change. *CLOmedia Online.* http://www.clomedia.com/departments/2003/December/349/index.php.

Davis, B. H., and J. P. Brewer. 1997. *Electronic Discourse: Linguistic Individuals in Virtual Space.* Albany, NY: State University of New York Press.

Edmondson, A. 1999. Psychological safety and learning behavior. *Administrative Science Quarterly* 44: 350–383.

———. 2003. Managing the risk of learning: Psychological safety in work teams. In *International handbook of organizational teamwork and cooperative working*, ed. M. A. West, D. Tjosvold, and K. G. Smith, 255–275. West Sussex, UK: John Wiley & Sons, Ltd.

Forrester, M. A. 1991. A conceptual framework for investigating learning in conversations. *Computers and Education* 17 (1): 61–72.

Gadamer, H. G. 1994. *Truth and method.* 2d rev. ed. New York: Crossroad.

Gibbs, G. R. 1999. Learning how to learn using a virtual learning environment for philosophy. *Journal of Computer Assisted Learning* 15: 221–231.

Griffith, T. L., J. E. Sawyer, and M. A. Neale. 2003. Virtualness and knowledge in teams: Managing the love triangle of organizations, individuals, and information technology. *MIS Quarterly* 27 (2): 265–287.

Hofstede, Geert H. 1997. *Culture and organizations: Software of the mind.* New York: McGraw-Hill.

Holsbrink-Engels, G. A. 1997. The effects of the use of a conversational model and opportunities for reflection in computer-based role-playing. *Computers in Human Behavior,* 13 (3): 409–436.

Horowitz, F., D. Bravington, and U. Silvis. 2006. The promise of virtual teams: Identifying key factors in effectiveness and failure. *Journal of European Industrial Training* 30 (6): 472–494.

Kimball, S. L., and J. Garrison. 1999. Hermeneutic listening in multicultural conversations. In *Affirming diversity through democratic conversations,* ed. V. R. Fu and A. J. Stremmel. Upper Saddle River, NJ: Merrill.

LaPorte, T. 2002. Technologies in/and culture, organization and politics. Unpublished paper. Arlington, VA: George Mason University School of Public Policy.

Lave, J., and E. Wenger. 1991. *Situated learning: Legitimate peripheral participation.* New York: Cambridge University Press.

McLoughlin, C. 1999. Culturally responsive technology use: Developing an on-line community of learners. *British Journal of Educational Technology* 30 (3): 231–243.

Newman, D., P. Griffen, and M. Cole. 1989. *The construction zone: Working for cognitive change in school.* London: Routledge.

Overholt, A. 2002. Virtually there? *Fast Company* 56: 108.

Pauleen, D., and P. Yoong. 2001. Facilitating virtual team relationships via Internet and conventional communication channels. *Internet Research* 11 (3): 190–202.

Richter, I. 1998. Individual and organizational learning at the executive level: Towards a research agenda. *Management Learning* 29: 299–316.

Rycroft, R. W., and D. E. Kash. 1999. *The complexity challenge: Technological innovation for the 21st century.* New York: Pinter.

Schrage, M. 1989. *No more teams!* New York: Doubleday.

Scott, J. 2000. Facilitating interorganizational learning with information technology. *Journal of Management Information Systems* 17 (2): 81–113.

Thomson Job Impact Study. 2002. The next generation of corporate learning: Achieving the right blend. http://www.delmarlearning.com/resources/job_impact_study_whitepaper.pdf.

van der Smagt, T. 2000. Enhancing virtual teams: Social relations v. communication technology. *Industrial Management & Data Systems* 100 (4): 148–156.

Weedman, J. 1999. Conversation and community: The potential of electronic conferences for creating intellectual proximity in distributed learning environments. *Journal of the American Society for Information Science* 50 (10): 907–928.

Williams, R. L. 1999. Managing an on-line community. *The Journal for Quality and Participation* 22 (6): 54–55.

8

Reflection as Movement

The combination of engagement and imagination results in a reflective practice. Such a practice combines the ability both to engage and to distance . . . Imagination enables us to adopt other perspectives . . . In turn, engagement provides a place for imagination *to land,* to be negotiated in practice and realized into identities of participation. . . . For instance, there is no point going on a retreat, a visit, or a sabbatical unless the new perspectives we gain in the process can find a realization in a new form of engagement upon our return. (emphasis added) (Wenger 1999, 217)

In talking about reflection, people often use phrases such as *stepping back* from a situation, *looking down* at it as if from above, and *going deeper* below the surface. Each invokes a sense of movement. Moving away from an experience, or *distancing* as Wenger puts it, may provide clarity, insight, and perspective. By stepping outside of an experience it is easier to slow it down enough to *understand* it in new ways; to see below the surface of spoken words and observable behaviors. Reflection is not inert. It is not passive. It is proactive, generative movement.

Imagination is similar. Imagination involves seeing new possibilities and acting on them. By reflecting on a current situation and becoming more aware of it, the imagination has a place to *land* (Wenger 1999). Once grounded, a person is better able to negotiate future life changes. Consequently, if there is a kind of work life or community in which we want to live, the change begins with internal and external reflection of the self and the environment, respectively.

Collective Reflective Practices

The required opening [for] participation is both personal and communal. Our identities must be able to absorb our new perspectives and make them part of who we are. (Wenger 1999, 217)

Reflective practices operate simultaneously on individual and communal levels. This chapter focuses on communal, collective reflection and reflective practices, partially because so much has already been written on individual reflection. Collective practices are complex, demanding processes and an essential element of changing organizations, which are social entities that necessitate collective reflection.

Individuals can engage in reflection and reflective practices alone, in dyadic relationships, and in groups of people who have shared interests. The distinction between reflection and reflective practices is not the number of people or size of the group but is the emphasis on *practice*. Collective reflective practices can be spontaneous though intentional times also need to be set aside for participants to integrate the individual with their collective imaginings and engagements. Through reflective practices people weave together their histories, current experiences, dreams, and imagination. Practice implies repeated behaviors that are incorporated deliberately into the rhythms of life. Practice gives people

> ... the scaffolding that leads [them] to discover this deeper understanding for [themselves]. . . . [Practice] derives from deeper principles that have been developed over time. In this sense it is not a recipe so much as a meditation: It requires constant repetition, over years, with the understanding that one will always be learning. A practice . . . usually arises in the context of a community . . . The community reinforces the necessity of the practice, supporting continuous reflection and improvement. (Isaacs 1999, 79–80)

In this context *reflective practice* refers to reflection that is intentionally incorporated into the ongoing flow of work life. A *community* refers to a group of people within an organization and across organizational and public life that intentionally recognizes the value of ongoing collective reflection to encourage continuous learning and improvement.

Communal reflection could, for example, be a project team that builds in regular, specific times for the team or subgroups to reflect on the original goals in light of subsequent developments and consider needs for revision. Groups reflect on elements of their work up to that point and ask what has been successful or unsuccessful. They engage their differing perspectives openly through catalytic conversations. They imagine alternatives and new possibilities. An emphasis on reflection, imagination, and catalytic conversations, as distinct from project management, is not to assess, complain, or mandate. Instead the focus is on learning from the engagements in an effort to alter and improve the work practice in light of new insights.

Such learning is also a dialogue between theory and practice. Participants look for connections between their conceptual understanding and practices so that the two inform each other. An ongoing dialogue between practice and theory is at the crux of what it means to be on the cutting edge and to be a learning organization, as distinct from incessantly missing opportunities, being reactive, and playing catch-up.

For previous experience to inform conceptual understanding and for the conceptual learning of theory to inform practice, there must be time for reflection. To learn from experience, people need to be alert to clues to recognize repetitive patterns, to surface their differences, and to consider new learning to inform future practice.

Cultural Influences

There are cultural differences that influence the degree to which people are disposed to reflection. As you began reading this chapter, did you have a visceral feeling of apprehension or anticipation knowing that the topic was reflection? Did you have thoughts or feelings that reflection is just not realistic in your life because of the pace or some other reason? Or did you feel that reflection is already a fundamental part of your life? Although there are certainly individual differences that influence such responses, cultural norms also strongly influence differing perceptions about the value of reflection. To clarify, my use of the word *cultural* is less defined by nation-state borders than by organizational and sociological influences such as religion or regional differences.

Western cultures in general, and the United States in particular, encourage accomplishing goals, achieving outcomes, producing results, and being efficient more than taking time for reflection. Imagine for a moment a typical workplace in the United States. What would be the most likely reaction of a boss who saw workers staring out of windows or sitting quietly in contemplation? In my experience these behaviors would probably be interpreted as wasting time. In many other parts of the world, the response might be sharply different. Some cultures encourage and value reflecting on life and living fully in the present moment as much or more than being efficient and accomplishing goals. A common colloquialism that describes this difference is that people in the United States seem to *live to work* while in many other cultures people *work to live*. The specific distinction is not whether work or living is valued. Instead it is one of priority. Does work take precedence or is having time outside of work a higher priority? It does not have to be one or the other.

Perceptions of time are part of this distinction and vary dramatically across cultures. In the United States, the priority given to achieving results is closely intertwined with a focus on time. People tend to perceive of time as an "irreversible sequence of seconds, minutes, hours, days, months, and years. . . . Once time is gone, you lose it forever" (Hampden-Turner and Trompenaars 2000, 295). Time within this frame of reference gets broken into sequential units to enable people to use it efficiently to accomplish goals. When those units are not productive, a common, often unconscious perception is that the time is not recoverable. For instance, time is allocated through appointments to maximize the efficient use of time and minimize "wasting" time to increase productivity.

People in cultures that tend to relate to time more synchronistically live within different frames of reference. Time is not perceived as segments that are used or lost as much as an entity that is cyclical, recurrent, and in tune with natural cycles of nature, such as seasonal and lunar cycles. *Good timing* takes precedence over *using time* to accomplish specific outcomes. Holding firm to prearranged schedules is less important than being responsive to the current situation. An underlying assumption is that it is difficult to predict the timeliness of meetings or events. Giving people more time if needed in the moment is a higher priority than meeting with more people during the course of a day or week. Thus, time with friends, family, and work colleagues is less scheduled, and the regenerative nature of beginnings and endings, of life and death, is prominent.

Reflective practices can take many shapes and forms, although to be *effective* they must be congruent with the culture and context and adapted as needed by the people involved. People oriented toward either of these extremes (i.e., not wasting time or continuously recurring time) may benefit by learning from each other. I suggest that there is a parallel between reflection and imagination, both of which entail some value for *good timing*. Similarly, there is a parallel between practice and engagement, especially at a communal level when incorporated into the rhythm of organizational life. Complementing reflection and imagination with practice and engagement can promote catalytic conversations, emergent knowledge, and innovation.

Reflection and Action Continuum

Practice and engagement are forms of action, and the parallels mentioned earlier bring to mind the dialectical continuum of reflection and action. Is reflection the opposite of taking action? According to the *Oxford English Dictionary* (2nd edition), common definitions of the word *reflection* are to look back, to refer back, to fix thoughts on some subject, and the image created in a mirror or similar polished object. Reflection can also be defined as the act of light or heat being thrown back or bending back onto a surface. It can refer to a meditation or deep contemplation. Embedded within the meaning of reflection though is its dialectical opposite—*action*. Whether perceived as one dialectical extreme or the other, as contemplation or throwing back, there is recursive movement as people recollect experiences, explore differing perspectives, and imagine alternatives to inform future actions and engagements. The dialectical tensions between these two extremes in group, organizational, and interorganizational life are at the heart of the remainder of this chapter.

Paulo Freire, a Brazilian educator and philosopher who was jailed and then exiled from his country in 1964 after a military coup, insisted that the transformation of the world had to begin with dialogue that must grow out of the synthesis of reflection and action.

> The insistence that the oppressed engage in reflection on their concrete situation is not a call to armchair revolution. On the contrary, reflection—true reflection—leads to action. On the other hand, when the situation calls for action, that action will constitute an authentic praxis only if its consequences become the object of critical reflection. (Freire 1992, 52–53)

For Freire, *praxis* is the nexus between reflection and action and the source of transformative change. Within true dialogue, "we find two dimensions, reflection and action, in such radical interaction that if one is sacrificed—even in part—the other immediately suffers" (Freire 1992, 75). Transformative dialogue depends on action that is informed by reflection to increase learning that influences future actions (see Figure 8.1). As action and reflection inform each other, the power of continuous learning and praxis is released.

When reflection does not grow out of action or lead to action, it is empty. In Freire's (1992) words, "When dialogue is deprived of its

Figure 8.1 **Praxis: the interface among reflection, learning, and action**

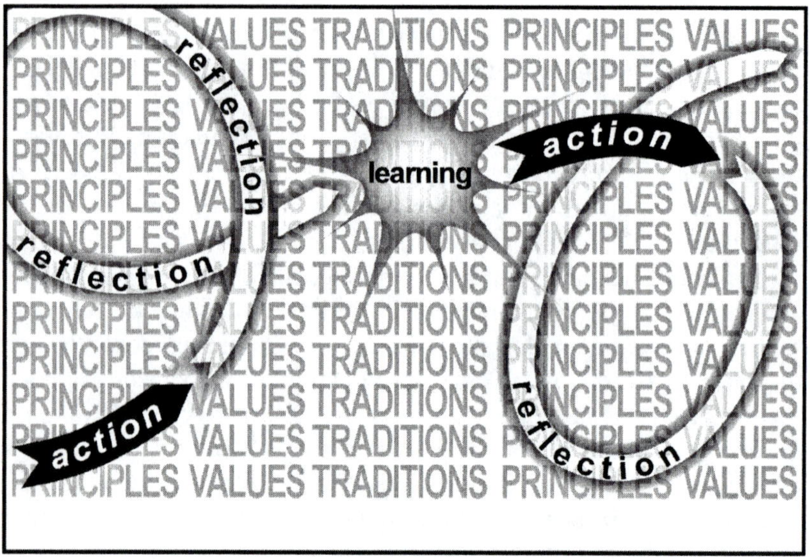

dimension of action, reflection automatically suffers as well; and [it] is changed into idle chatter, into *verbalism,* into an alienated and alienating 'blah.' It becomes . . . empty" (p. 75–76). Thus, when reflection is disassociated from action, it takes on an indulgent character that can easily become alienated from the world and be useless.

The reverse is similarly devoid of power. "[I]f action is emphasized exclusively, to the detriment of reflection, . . . [dialogue] is converted into . . . action for action's sake—negates the true praxis and makes dialogue impossible" (Freire 1992, 76). For action to have substance, for it to be congruent with larger principles and values, for it to be connected to valued historical traditions while also moving toward a preferred future, the activity must be grounded through conscientious reflective practices. It is within this creative tension that reflection acts as a source of dialogue, movement, and transformational change.

Reflection Is Essential Because . . .

Incessant action, without time for reflection, functions like a shield or a barrier to learning by filling the available time and space. Action can be a powerful distracter. It can be perpetuated unconsciously because the activity is such a part of the lexicon of habitual behaviors. Scheduling appointments back to back with no time for spontaneity during or between them is an everyday example of incessant action. Taking on more new projects than a person can possibly do well and then holding onto all of the work and decision making without bringing in other interested people is another example. Incessant activity reinforces the perception that there is no time for brainstorming, retreat, or other kinds of collective reflection.

As illustrated in Figure 8.2, incessant actions serve as a shield to keep us disconnected from a variety of phenomena that are actually essential elements of learning and regenerative change in the contemporary world. Incessant action helps people avoid grappling with the pervasive ambiguity associated with complexity. Incessant action does not eliminate the ambiguity—or the complexity—but it holds it below the surface of consciousness. Without reflection on our practices, ambiguous causes and consequences of daily problems and issues are ignored as projects go forward as planned. Avoiding ambiguity feeds instinctive efforts to try to create predictability and maintain control. The ambiguity that lies below the surface hides the sources of tension and creates pervasive unsettledness.

Incessant action can also prevent the questioning of assumptions and making changes. By not questioning assumptions, people limit their options exponentially. Prevailing, operating assumptions in organizations operate like phyla in biology that provide a place to file all variations of creatures, such as Mollusca (mollusks) or Arthropoda (arthropods). Prevailing assumptions operate in organizational life as categories within which to organize seemingly overwhelming amounts of information and alternative behaviors. By grouping according to similarity, much of life's rich diversity is erased, thus stifling imagination (Weick 2005), creativity, and change.

The predilection for action can insulate people from being aware of and grappling with layers of differences and complexity. It can interfere with the capacity to recognize changes that are going to affect them and their organizations. Walking a seemingly comfortable path and not seeing complexity and impending change leaves people and organizations vulnerable. On the other hand, organizations can intentionally integrate reflective practices and opportunities for emergent conversations to uncover complexity and make it easier to anticipate possibilities.

Figure 8.2   **Shield of incessant action**

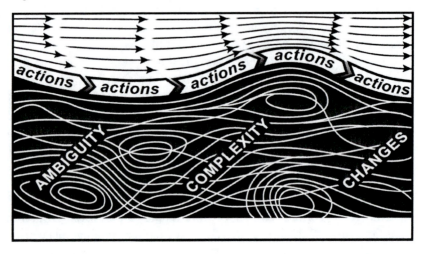

The Ability to Respond

Whether it occurs naturally or deliberately, by its very nature, reflection slows down the pace of organizational life. Speed often provokes reactions. There is not enough time to consider subtleties, new information, and unintended consequences. Speed limits the time available to anticipate the impact of a choice of words or the tone used. It contributes to oversimplification. An overemphasis on speed and efficiency also makes it more difficult to develop relationships because they take time. Speed minimizes the sharing of diverse points of view and discourages the surfacing of differing perspectives. There is more pressure for assimilation of differences into the status quo rather than surfacing and exploring the differences as catalysts for learning and changes to improve collective actions.

With collaborative interactions, the nature of complex environments is more easily recognized, and the concept of responsibility changes to mean having the *ability to respond*. Collaborative, reflective, less hierarchical settings can promote the development of shared commitment among people to the quality and timeliness of work. In many settings, people who have ongoing contact are prone to feel they are answerable to one another rather than to a more distant, unknown authority figure. A self-organizing sense of responsibility emerges. Responsibility becomes more systemically incorporated into the context rather than requiring external enforcement.

Let me give you an example of varying forms of responsibility. Think about the ways people make decisions in a specific organizational setting that you know well. First, do decisions actually get made? If so, who makes them? Does one person or a small group of people make decisions? Or is there broad input? Do decision makers gather information and ideas to inform their decisions? If so, do they gather substantial information from diverse sources? The answers to these kinds of questions help to reveal the organizational patterns of decision-making processes. The norms that shape expectations and perpetuate these processes can become the structures within which people behave. When people begin to question the norms and imagine new possibilities, their frames of reference extend beyond the familiar psychic filing or categorizing systems—i.e., the origin of the phrase "thinking outside of the box." They begin to see that the boundaries around the categories often can be porous or movable. Things can be done differently. For example, early in the planning process the organization can seek and then use wider input to guide organizational or project priorities.

Large amounts of data and information barrage people in organizations, and so the tendency is to organize new information into categories that are familiar and accepted in that context, thus limiting imagination and alternative options. Unconscious categories or boxes help people keep track of fast-moving behaviors in organizations while also discouraging imagination and minimizing the likelihood of picking up on clues to changes (Weick 2005). To think outside of the box, to be imaginative, requires the hard work of breaking habits, creating new categories, and enlisting support for these new ways of seeing the world. It may seem on the surface that it saves the organization time to continue former patterns and not to challenge the status quo. Yet stakeholders need to question whether the status quo serves the organization, especially over the long term. What is the cost in terms of quality of performance, long-term viability, credibility among diverse stakeholders, and life for people affected by the current procedures, decisions, and subsequent behaviors? In the short term, it may appear adequate. The question is whether the organization and the individual stakeholders are missing opportunities or are blind to serious threats as a result of a lack of imagination and limiting input and priority setting to a narrow group of actors at the top. For example, Weick (2005) describes how even though there were many clues to the terrorist attacks of September 11, 2001, the value of the information was not recognized because of a "failure of imagination."

People who engage in collective reflective practices on an ongoing basis are more likely to bring in more data, recognize subtle shifts, anticipate change, and be innovative. Collective reflection alone is not the answer, although it is a key element of the enabling environment. What does it take for an organization to have the *ability to respond* differently and to shift the weight of responsibility more broadly? It entails having the flexibility to move in new directions and feeling personally committed enough to want to respond. Let me discuss some ways to facilitate helpful patterns.

Enabling Conditions for Collective Reflective Practices

Although collective reflective practices can take many forms, conversation is the primary medium through which people learn, and often it is in reflecting with others that fundamental shifts occur. I suggest six enabling conditions that are especially relevant to collective reflective practices:

- Relationships based on mutual respect
- Relationships based on mutual trust and psychological safety
- Recognition and acknowledgment of the benefits of participation
- Inclusive decision making about time devoted to reflective practices and to the shape and forms they take
- Time devoted to reflection on short-term and long-term implications
- Inclusion of individual reflection to complement collective reflection

Figure 8.3 illustrates these dynamics. In the text, I elaborate primarily on the first two enabling conditions and briefly mention the other less complex ideas.

Elements of vulnerability and risk are unavoidable when people engage in genuine, substantive learning and development. Acknowledging mistakes, asking questions, asking for help, mulling over feedback, giving constructive feedback, listening to learn, asking questions in ways that demonstrate good intentions, and debriefing experiences to maximize learning are all components of learning from experience. They become the medium through which people improve competencies,

Figure 8.3 **Enabling conditions for collective reflective practices**

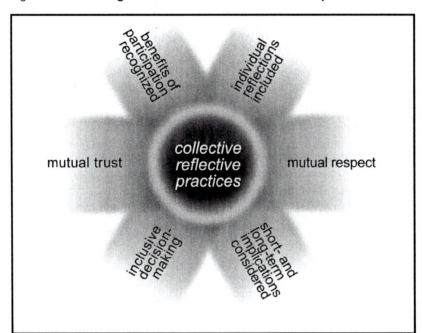

skills, effectiveness, and quality. These behaviors involve risk taking as they expose people's vulnerabilities. The first two enabling conditions address these issues.

Mutual Respect

Collective reflective practices depend on mutual respect. Because groups need to create their own norms for acceptable behavior, to me there are very few nonnegotiable norms; however, respect is nonnegotiable. Respect does not require agreement with, support of, or fondness for another person or group. It does, however, require accepting, acknowledging, and listening to the other party. It involves making concentrated efforts to interact in a mode of inquiry and with consideration of other people's feelings.

Isaacs (1999) says that when respect is lacking, people begin to impose themselves on others and try to change them. He says that,

> To respect someone is to look for the springs that feed the pool of their experience. The word comes from the Latin *respecere,* which means 'to look again.' Its most ancient roots mean 'to observe.' It involves a sense of honoring or deferring to someone. Where once we saw one aspect of a person, we look again and realize how much of them we had missed. . . . At its core, the act of respect invites us to see others as *legitimate.* (p. 110–111)

When we are not willing to *look again* to try to understand more fully what a person is saying and valuing, we narrow the space for conversation and chances for learning; we also cut off opportunities for inquiry. Without respect, it is easy to shift into advocacy by trying to make our perspective the *right* one and to make the other perspective *wrong.* We are then not recognizing the complexity of the other or honoring this other's legitimacy. Instead we pigeonhole this other person to fit into a box or category that is fixed in our minds.

Mutual respect is so vital that disrespect becomes a toxic force in a group or an organization. When a person or group is treated disrespectfully, it makes other people apprehensive and much more reluctant to be vulnerable in that context. When a member of a group is belittled, punished, or embarrassed for making a well-intentioned mistake or is not given the benefit of the doubt, generally a stifling cloud of caution settles over the group. This is especially true if the offender is in a position of power, for example, the manager. Sometimes the behavior degenerates into angry, disrespectful retorts or behind-the-scenes sabotage. This behavior curtails, if not eliminates, open reflection, learning, and risk taking. Respect is more than passive acceptance. It calls for active intention.

Trust and Psychological Safety

All except the most routine jobs in knowledge-intensive economies require continuous learning and improvement. Feedback is a critical element of learning, refers to previous experiences, and involves reflection. Debriefing is a collective form of reflection. Asking questions and asking for help generally emerge out of reflection or anticipation about gaps in knowledge or competence.

Even new responsibilities involve reflection for learning. For example, if I accept a new responsibility, I need to think about, or reflect on, previous similar work, my observations of others engaged in related work, and ways that I feel prepared and unprepared. To improve my competence, I need to stretch myself to develop new abilities. The consequences that I expect strongly influence how open I am about these needs, how much help I seek, and whom I approach, if anyone. My sense of trust and psychological safety inform my expectations and behavior and hence also influence my readiness to engage in collective reflective practices.

Trust and psychological safety are increasingly relevant and common topics in organizational settings and related research. Although the terms trust and psychological safety are complementary, they are not interchangeable. Edmondson (2003) explicates these distinctions especially well. She says that while trust and psychological safety are both intrapsychic perceptions and involve vulnerability and concern about consequences, the differences between the two are important. Trust is part of a dyadic relationship, while psychological safety is shaped by interpersonal relationships among people, such as members of a team. In other words, a relationship of trust is with one other person or group while psychological safety applies to group members in an ongoing relationship.

Another difference is that "trust involves giving others the benefit of the doubt—indicating a focus on others' potential actions or trustworthiness. . . . [I]n psychological safety, the question is whether others will give you the benefit of the doubt when you have made a mistake or asked an apparently stupid question" (Edmondson 2003, 259). In other words, if I trust a person, I give them the benefit of the doubt. Psychological safety involves expectations about whether other group members will give me the benefit of the doubt if I blunder.

A third distinction is that while trust can be related to expectations about short- or long-term consequences, psychological safety is a perception about more immediate expectations and consequences. Therefore, if I am a member of a group that currently shares a considerable degree of psychological safety, it will feel less risky to reveal my vulnerabilities by asking for help because the previous pattern was not to embarrass or punish other team members for similar behavior. Teams with high psychological safety are much more likely to admit mistakes and ask for help than teams with low psychological safety (Edmondson 1996, 1999). I propose that they are also more conducive to collective reflection and imagination. As people recall their perceptions, experiences, and feelings in front of others, mutual trust and psychological safety reduce the sense of vulnerability. As people imagine new, untried possibilities, they likewise can feel more confident that they will not be discounted or embarrassed.

Other Enabling Conditions

The other four factors similarly work in tandem. All participants need to have input in decisions related to their collective reflective practices, such as the amount of time used for the practices, how often they will occur, and the format. Inclusive decision making increases the likelihood that collective reflective practices will add value for participants and the organization. Moreover, approaches that work well in one context need to be tailored to another, and the input guides the adaptations. Participants help decide who will be involved, what people will do, and how to encourage spontaneous collective reflections.

Participants' awareness of the benefits of reflective practices is the fourth enabling condition and is closely related to their input. As is often the case, the more that people are involved in the planning, project, and creation of a practice, the more likely it is to add value to the practice or plan and the more likely they are to feel committed to it.

Because short-term goals drive most fast-moving organizations, collective reflective practices offer rare opportunities for consideration of the longer-term consequences of organizational decisions and actions. The intent is not that the long-term perspective should replace the short-term. Instead, complementing the short-term with consideration for long-term implications minimizes unintended consequences and improves organizational decision making.

Recognizing the inseparable nature of self-awareness and group effectiveness leads to the sixth enabling condition. Within the collective reflection practices format, there should be time for individual reflection, prompting the introduction of invaluable individual insight directly into the milieu. Individual reflection can facilitate the transition from work to collective reflection. In addition, heightening self-awareness generally contributes to the value of the collective work by encouraging Schon's *reflective practitioner* to take residence in the organization.

The Shape of Reflection

By shape, I mean the design, format, and venue of collective reflective practice sessions—that is, what people are doing, what the activities would look and sound like, where people are. Considerations such as the degree to which sessions are structured, unstructured, formal, or informal are all part of the shape. All of these decisions depend on the local setting or context, the intentions and purposes, and the experience and attitudes that people have about reflection.

The possible formats of reflective practices are limited only by the imagination. Opening with time for individual reflection through personal writing or quiet time can help participants shift from the routines and hustle of work. The caveat is to be sure that people feel no pressure to share their personal thoughts or writing unless they choose to do so. It is critical to honor personal privacy. If not, people will be preoccupied planning what to say publicly during individual reflection time in subsequent collective sessions, thus undermining the purpose.

The collective reflection time can include one-on-one conversations, small group conversations, and/or large group conversations. The interactions can be relatively spontaneous and informal if the environment allows, or they may be formal and planned. A few distinctions that differentiate between informal and formal involve the amount of preplanning, the amount of structure to the conversations, and the degree to which spontaneity is possible.

More formal reflective practices are often held at a regularly scheduled time, such as once a month or twice a year, with a well-planned agenda shared with participants prior to the event. An important warning is needed here: If the agenda or activities in the sessions become a time for reports or monologues, then it is not a reflective practice and should not be represented as such. If the leadership or planning group calls an event reflective when it is not, the behavior undermines their credibility and congruence (i.e., not walking the talk) and misrepresents the nature of reflection.

Structure can take various forms. Structured sessions are more likely to be facilitated, preferably by an outside facilitator to enable all regular members to participate fully. Structure may also include specific plans for ways to engage everyone in active reflection. For instance, the facilitator may pose open-ended questions to the group and encourage everyone to comment. Or the facilitator might ask people to reflect individually on an event, high point, or low point of the group's work in the recent past. After the personal reflection time, people can be asked to pair up or form trios and share whatever they are comfortable saying to each other. People can be assigned to specific groups or be asked to create their own groups. When people do not know each other or have difficulty working with one another, assigning people to groups may be preferable. If people are resistant to the process, then allowing them to select their group members is helpful by giving them more control over their participation.

After the pairs or trios have talked, each one can join another pair or trio for further conversation, or everyone can be brought back together into the large group, depending on the size of the group and how challenging it may be for people to talk about these reflections. Rather than having reports, I usually suggest more spontaneous sharing in the large group to allow conversations to emerge. As group size increases, people need even more flexibility with regard to how much they want to share in the larger group as size of group strongly affects comfort level for many people.

An unstructured reflection, on the other hand, would open with little or no specific format or agenda to get people to talk. This reflection may or may not have a facilitator. Unless the group has extensive experience with collective reflective practices and a high degree of psychological safety, I do not recommend unstructured reflection sessions without a facilitator because unconstructive behavior can develop and be damaging to individuals, groups, and organizations. Preferably, facilitators know either the group or the kind of group, have credibility with the participants, are well-versed in group dynamics, and are able to gauge their interventions appropriately between being too laissez faire or too controlling. The selection of the facilitators is critical; they need to be well-trained and experienced or work with experienced co-facilitators. Another valuable benefit of training group members as facilitators is that they can encourage spontaneous reflection and the constructive surfacing of differences and conflict resolution on an ongoing basis.

With structured time, it is easier to guide the conversation toward especially important topics, to encourage constructive reflection, and to increase the opportunities for more people to talk in small groups. The downsides are that topics and feelings that are hard to talk about can be more easily avoided because the time is filled by structured activities and staying on task. A tight structure limits people from pursuing topics that emerge during discussion and need more time to address. It can also increase resistance when participants do not feel as though they had adequate input into shaping the experience.

The more structured the design, the less open time and spontaneity are available. Straddling the fine line between too much and too little structure is challenging. The context and the purpose clearly need to guide these decisions. Involving participants in the planning process, led by people seasoned with collective reflection experience, is a valuable way to gauge this fine line between structure and spontaneity because these nuanced decisions improve the quality of the interactions exponentially.

Reflections can be integrated into already occurring events, such as retreats, staff meetings, and project debriefings. They can be specifically included at the beginning of new projects and built in at various stages during project implementation to encourage ongoing learning and improvement of the work. If enabling conditions for quality conversational space are in place, it is relatively easy to encourage people to self-organize into spontaneous reflection and trust them to use time wisely. Access to appropriate physical space and group members with facilitation expertise further support spontaneous self-organizing reflections.

The Substance of Reflection

The substance of reflection is the content and topics about which people reflect and talk. The potential content, whether collective or individual, is vast. The local context, purposes, experience, and attitudes guide and determine the content. For example, in my own experience working in higher education within state government in the United States, sometimes reflective practices worked well and sometimes we could have used more reflection.

I entered the agency as one of two associate directors. The small staff and I worked together closely on many projects to which we were deeply committed and in which we believed. One of our achievements was acquiring considerable grant money. These funds gave us leverage and influence and allowed us to bring in more staff and encourage other organizations to work with us. After the executive director retired, I replaced him.

Overall, many of the enabling conditions for using reflective practices were in place when I became the director. People knew each other well, respected each other, and shared many common values; there was a good bit of trust and psychological safety. People generally wanted to be included in the conversations about planning and implementation although the extremely demanding pace of the work made time a major obstacle.

Moreover, we conducted much of the work outside of the office setting, meaning that coordinating schedules required intentional planning and effort. It also meant people had to believe that it would be worth their time and effort to participate. With the previous director, the professional staff members had regular conversations although the director made the decisions, giving others little recourse for reconsideration. Support staff was never included in those conversations and therefore had no formal experience with collective reflection.

One of the first things I did as the new director was to remove the sofas in my new office and replace them with a round table and chairs that would accommodate all of the primary staff. We decided together as a staff on a time for holding weekly staff meetings, which can be a good opportunity for collective reflection and imagination. In retrospect, however, I am not sure we ever seriously considered whether we needed weekly meetings.

We had several practices that facilitated bringing a wide range of possible actions to the group. For example, different people had responsibility for monitoring possible new sources of grant money, and we shared these potential opportunities as a regular part of weekly meetings. Each person also had time in the meetings to bring up other topics, issues, and opportunities. We were a diverse group with different networks and thus had access to information about various possibilities and feedback for overall work quality improvement. Moreover, ideas that came up during the work week were readily brought before the group for consideration. Overall, the group was effective at thinking outside of the box and incorporating short-term collective reflection, debriefing opportunities, obstacles, and events of the week.

We developed patterns of informal debriefing, such as in the halls, over coffee, in the parking lot immediately after events, and spontaneously at other times. When issues arose or decisions were being made, the group frequently brought up previous experiences and considered them in light of the current issues fairly thoroughly. However, I think that we leaned too heavily on allowing past experiences to shape our expectations, thus blinding ourselves to unusual possibilities and threats on the horizon.

Although most of the staff had good observation skills and tended to be reflective, we did not intentionally reach outside of our office to gather enough new perspectives and information from a wide range of people. For example, we did not specifically design dialogues for our varied stakeholders. If we had reflected more on subtle interconnections among them, we would have benefited and might have prevented serious problems. Group members anticipated and debriefed short-term problems and obstacles primarily because each person felt comfortable bringing them up and talking openly. We did not, however, have off-site, brainstorming sessions for more long-term reflection. If I were in that position now, I would have off-site sessions several times a year, attended by the entire staff. If we had also brought in some key outside stakeholders for parts of these sessions, we might have been able to see more accurately some of the external dynamics at play that would influence our effectiveness and future.

Demographically the staff was diverse, though not to the greatest extent. In terms of including everyone's voice among the staff and really listening to each other, I think that we did an outstanding job. The support staff let me know they would like to be included in some of the staff meetings. We included them and found their input invaluable. People felt safe enough to raise concerns and vulnerabilities either in the group reflection or one on one. Though my predisposition was to focus heavily on immediate work demands, I always encouraged people to let me know if they wanted to talk to me in private. When someone asked to talk, I always made time to meet within a few days, or sooner if they requested it or if I sensed that it was an urgent matter. I took performance appraisals seriously and invited open conversation about wide-ranging issues during those sessions. During these reviews, I deliberately slowed the pace and asked open-ended questions of the support staff and professional staff about their feelings, recent experiences, and what they wanted to be doing in the future.

We talked openly about whether continuation of existing projects or new projects was consistent with our personal and organizational values. We sought congruence, recognizing that, while we shared many values, our priorities sometimes varied.

We frequently had open conversations about the meaning of actions and behaviors. When people made observations that surprised me, I generally remembered that the perceptions of others are just as important, if not more important, than my own. Coincidentally, shortly after becoming the director, I participated in an off-site leadership development program that included 360-degree feedback on my performance. I asked most of the members of the staff to complete confidential assessments of my work, style, and so on, and return them to an external third party.

Figure 8.4   **Reflection-action and imagination-engagement dialectics**

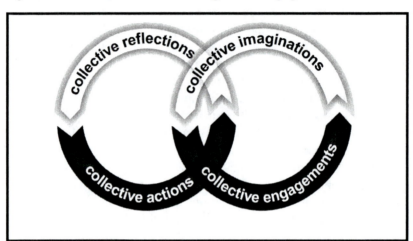

As part of that program, I received extensive feedback, some of which came from these staff assessments.

Several things surprised me. One was that people wanted more direction from me. My perception had been that I respected and trusted the staff so fully that I assumed they did not want or need any more direction than I was already giving. Another surprise was that one person said that I had become too serious since becoming the director and wanted me to lighten up and regain my sense of humor. Even then, I realized how fortunate I was to have that kind of feedback early in my tenure. I was able to address these and other concerns and to become much more sensitive to similar issues. I also used the feedback to open further conversations by having numerous one-on-one conversations. I shared the essence of some of the feedback and asked if they wanted to elaborate. These conversations led to considerable learning and better relationships.

Conclusions

Shared engagements among stakeholders can constructively feed their collective imaginations, as illustrated in Figure 8.4. This dialectic also relates closely to the reflection-action dialectic.

In the same way that reflection and action need to inform each other for learning and systemic change, encouraging imagination makes it possible to gain invaluable new perspectives to improve engagements. Current engagements can be enriched by incorporating collective imagination into collective reflection. Wenger suggests that our imaginations and dreams need a place to land. As they land in our engagements, they prompt, catalyze, and enliven our work and improve organizational potential.

References

Edmondson, A. 1996. Learning from mistakes is easier said than done: Group and organizational influences on the detection and correction of human error. *Journal of Applied Behavioral Science* 32: 5–28.

———. 1999. Psychological safety and learning behavior. *Administrative Science Quarterly* 44: 350–383.

———. 2003. Managing the risk of learning: Psychological safety in work teams. In *International handbook of organizational teamwork and cooperative working*, ed. M. A. West, D. Tjosvold, and K. G. Smith, 255–275. West Sussex, England: John Wiley & Sons, Ltd.

Freire, P. 1992. *Pedagogy of the oppressed*. New York: Continuum.

Hampden-Turner, C. M., and F. Trompenaars. 2000. *Building cross-cultural competence: How to create wealth from conflicting values*. New Haven, CT: Yale University Press.

Isaacs, W. 1999. *Dialogue and the art of thinking together*. New York: Currency.

Weick, K. E. 2005. Organizing and failure of imagination. *International Public Management Journal* 8 (3): 425–438.

Wenger, E. 1999. *Communities of practice: Learning, meaning, and identity*. New York: Cambridge University Press.

9

What's in a Story?

Larry Prusak, the former executive director of IBM's Institute of Knowledge Management and a leading author and consultant in knowledge management, says that since the beginning of the twenty-first century he has seen,

> . . . stories becoming more valuable, because, slowly but surely, knowledge is increasingly the source of wealth, especially in Western and Asian nations. And if knowledge is a source of wealth, rather than land, labor and capital, or more physical attributes, one of the ways knowledge is configured and transferred is through stories. (Brown et al. 2004, 45)

Focusing on stories and narrative is a natural progression from the previous discussion on collective reflection. Stories are a form of conversation and stories among diverse participants are like catalytic conversations. An organization's knowledge is embedded in its people, who bring with them an amalgamation of differing kinds of expertise and wide-ranging interpretations. These resources enter the collective environment through conversations and often through the sharing of stories and narrative accounts.

Take a moment to remember times when you were in a group of people telling stories about their experiences, such as "When that happened . . ." or "You will not believe how my department . . ." kinds of stories. One person shares a story that reminds others of something similar. One story leads to another usually in an irregular, unpredictable fashion. Even when people are not consciously aware of this conversational pattern, they are participating in human behavior that goes back to oral traditions prior to written communication. Stories often pepper conversations as people interact in work groups, during social times with friends, and in community, religious, and family groups.

What Qualifies as a "Story" Here?

Story is one of the words used to define *narrative,* and the reverse can also be true (*Oxford English Dictionary,* 2nd edition). The etymology of both words includes elements of history and accounts of events. Both words involve making connections, through events or emotions, to decipher meaning. Although I use the words interchangeably in some cases, *story* invokes a more commonplace and informal interaction than *narrative,* which is sometimes associated with literary accounts. The mediums for each are conversation or written text.

Stories are ubiquitous and permeate organizational life. They thread through conversations as people recall things that have happened, illustrate a point, or communicate values. For example,

- "During the staff meeting last week . . ."
- "One time when he was on a trip . . ."
- "Every time we have a crisis . . ."

Stories recall the origins, or historical roots, of groups and organizations:

- "So the story goes, the founder came from . . ."
- "From the very beginning, this group . . ."

Stories provide examples as guides for the future:

- "I found out the hard way how important it is here when . . ."

In this way, stories are immediate even when they are about a distant time and place. Stories that live on as people repeat them over time are grounded in common experience. It is often in hearing stories of the experiences of others that participants recognize new parts of themselves. Thus, the meaning that a person takes away from a story may not be what the storyteller intended. Instead, the stories connect with personal memories, feelings, fears, and joys and awaken new awareness. Listeners take and leave elements, depending on their own readiness. Stories are more inclusive and potent when they provide leeway for listeners to find their own way into the story to draw their own conclusions.

Stories that are especially remembered and influential are about unfolding events and tend to be nonjudgmental. They are inviting and not threatening. They can help people save face because the story as a rule is not about a listener, and admonitions often come through images. Although the message may be clear, listeners retain control of what it means to them.

The stand-up comic or the lone storyteller is not what I mean by storytelling in this chapter. Nor is the CEO's review of a sequence of events to a large group from behind a podium. Stories are interactive; they are not monologues. Rather, stories are dynamic, as listeners share, ask questions, chime in, and engage in nonverbal nodding and other gestures. The give and take gives rise to spontaneous, unpredictable possibilities.

Excessive organizational structure, formality, and adherence to procedure are stultifying and can numb the mind. Storytelling to open the imagination is analogous to taking time for warm-up exercises before strenuous physical activity. In the same way that we limber up the physical body so that it moves more easily to accomplish wider ranges of motion, organizations need to awaken these imaginative qualities of the psyche. This kind of mental limbering up can take a little time and effort to become more flexible. When the "image-creating" part of one's being and the images of memory are tapped, thinking processes loosen. It becomes easier to break out of rigid patterns and categorical ways of thinking.

The storytelling that I explore here is not the tall tale of yore as much as it is about people recounting their concrete experiences, coupled with their feelings (see Figure 9.1). Telling stories is retrospective, as the storyteller draws upon previous experiences, and prospective, as listeners are pulled forward to imagine unfamiliar possibilities. No matter how much stories are based on concrete experiences, the storytellers and engaged listeners enter the realm of imagination together.

Wenger (1998), a prominent spokesperson in knowledge management and organizational learning, talks about these dynamics as being pivotal. He says, "stories . . . allow us to enter the events, the characters, and their plights by calling upon our imagination. Stories can transport our experience into the situations they relate and involve us in producing the meanings of those events as though we were participants. As a result, they can be integrated into our identities and remembered as personal experience, rather than as mere reification. It is this ability to enable negotiability through imagina-

Figure 9.1 **Storytelling environment**

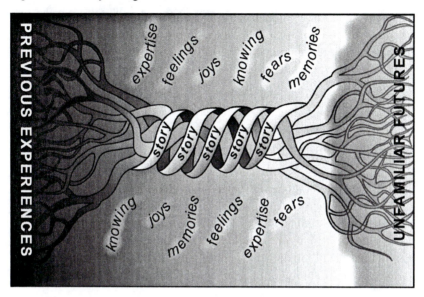

tion that makes stories, parables, and fables powerful communication devices" (p. 203–204).

Modes of Cognitive Functioning—Ways of Thinking

The following quote comes from a fictional account of life among the Mundo people in Mexico, people who are indigenous Indians and Blacks in an Alice Walker novel. Through the words of two of her characters, Walker (1998) eloquently expresses the complementary relationship of rational, conceptual language and stories. Listen to her words:

> "No one among the Mundo believes there is anyone on earth who truly knows anything about why we are here, Señor. To even have an idea about it would require a very big brain. A computer. That is why, instead of ideas, the Mundo have stories."
>
> "You are saying . . . that stories have more room in them than ideas? . . ."
>
> "That is correct, Señor. It is as if ideas are made of blocks. Rigid and hard. And stories are made of a gauze that is elastic. You can almost see through it, so what is beyond is tantalizing. You can't quite make it out; and because the imagination is always moving forward, you yourself are constantly stretching. Stories are the way spirit is exercised."

"But surely your people have ideas," I said.
"Of course we do. But we know there is a limit to them. After that, story!"
(pp. 193–194)

Walker's metaphor of stories as elastic, like gauze, brings to mind how stories tantalizingly draw listeners in to see beyond and through them as they awaken memories and imagination. Unlike the abstract language of ideas that serves many communication needs, narrative accounts and stories create images and open listeners' and readers' minds in other, equally valuable ways. Stories tend to reach out, almost as if somehow appending themselves to listeners' memories, experiences, thoughts, and feelings. Images emerge in the mind's eye as listeners make connections. Sometimes the links are so direct that listeners join the conversation, sharing their stories. Other times listeners will hold their reflections and imaginations inside. Whether the musings are verbalized or not, listeners take in the strands of the story lines that have meaning for them in that moment, at that time in their lives.

Conversations that focus on ideas and storytelling conversations are invaluable as they literally tap different parts of the brain. They tend to affect listeners in disparate ways.

> There are two modes of cognitive functioning, two modes of thought, each providing distinctive ways of ordering experience, of constructing reality. . . . A good story and a well-formed argument are different natural kinds. Both can be used as means for convincing another. Yet what they convince of is fundamentally different: arguments convince one of their truth, stories of their lifelikeness. (Bruner 1986, 11)

Within this one quote, Bruner draws attention to two polarities that set the stage for this chapter. He describes one polarity as the two modes of cognitive functioning—i.e., the good story and the well-formed argu-ment. The second polarity becomes apparent when he asks the reader to take into account where each approach leads—i.e., to truth or lifelikeness. In other words, what is the intention, the purpose?

Using Argument, Stories, or Both?

Each of these natural modes of thought, the argument and the story, is an essential part of organizational and personal communication, although they serve strikingly different purposes and move conversations in distinctly different directions. Whether a person is working through a performance appraisal in the workplace or parenting a teenager, logical, well-formed rationales are beneficial. Similarly, sharing experiences through stories often helps people in ongoing relationships understand each other better and become more invested in working together toward mutually decided goals. The two modes of thought are not mutually exclusive and may be complementary and positively reinforcing.

For example, if a manager is in a performance evaluation with an employee who needs to develop new competencies, multiple approaches are possible. If the manager directs the employee to take specific training courses without explaining or asking for the employee's input, the likely responses are passive compliance or resistance. Another approach is for the manager to share a story that illustrates a similar situation in which someone benefited from developing these competencies and follows up by asking for input. In the process of informal storytelling and open-ended questions, the employee feels less resistant, thereby opening the space for a give and take through which to invest in new learning. As Bruner (1990) says, it can "promote negotiation."

In some workplaces, developing well-formed arguments to influence others is the well-established norm. Especially in environments where analysis, logic, and efficiency are highly valued, debate and skillful argumentation may be the prevailing communication style. Although this approach is valuable, it does not promote interpersonal negotiation or the building of increased, mutual understanding and trust among people. At the same time, I propose that reliance on either well-formed arguments or good stories to the exclusion of the other is unwise, particularly in organizational life. Stakeholders with a wide repertoire of competencies can be more flexible and adapt more readily to changing circumstances; if only one approach is used, people may scorn others.

As you think about organizational and work environments that are familiar to you, is making a logical argument or sharing a story held in higher esteem? Are both equally valued? When one of the two dominates, common by-products are the exclusion of diverse people, squelching of innovation, and narrowing of prospects for substantial adaptation and change. When one type of narrative overly dominates, workspaces and conversational spaces often are uninviting to people with different styles and strengths.

The language used plays a role as well. People often express their preference for argument or stories in dichotomous, oppositional terms. For instance, they may venerate the objective while scorning the subjective, applaud the positivist or scientific while putting down the interpretive or postmodern. Other extremes include the abstract or context-based, comprehensive or apprehensive, cognitive or affective, left brain or right brain, episodic memory or semantic memory, digital cognition or analog cognition (Gadamer 1994; James 1890, 1977; Kolb 1984; Tulving 1983; van Maanen 1995; Vitz 1990). The use of strong dichotomous terms gives status to one extreme while undervaluing the other. Even though the terms are labels for complex concepts, overvaluing one side of a dichotomy to the disservice of the other reinforces rigidity in either direction.

Organizational norms that genuinely reward and demonstrate a value for multiple kinds of cognitive functioning are congruent with flexible environments that can tap broader ranges of talent. For instance, when empirical evidence is expected to back up a proposal made to a decision-making body, a logical well-formed argument with solid data is needed. Gathering facts and seeking empirical evidence are critical. Nonetheless, this approach represents only one mode of ordering thought, cognitive functioning, and grasping the complexity of organizational life. The proposal might also include a brief story to illustrate possible implications of implementation to increase its effectiveness. This technique is often used by lawyers, politicians, and the media: Lawyers tell stories in closing statements; in the State of the Union address, the president of the United States tells stories about individuals affected by government policies and introduces them to Congress and the television audience; and newspaper articles illustrate trends by featuring individual examples. Including illustrations of likely impacts on particular individuals or groups is a legitimate consideration that needs to be a part of decision-making, policy-setting, and planning processes.

Organizational stakeholders, by definition, cumulatively have diverse perspectives and associated priorities. When they are at odds with each other and locked in opposition, their conflicting perspectives impede their work and damage their self and shared interests. Rather than suppressing or drowning out other stakeholders, getting people to talk together and share stories can diffuse tension and opposition. Even more importantly, by bringing people's differences to the surface and sharing their varied interpretations, new data become available. Each person's version and description offers a fuller picture of the complex organizational and interorganizational landscapes. As people share their varied interpretations, it can "have the effect of framing the idiosyncratic in a 'lifelike' fashion that can promote negotiation and avoid confrontational disruption and strife. . . . differences in meaning can be resolved by invoking mitigating circumstances that account for divergent interpretations of 'reality'" (Bruner 1990, 67). In other words, stories give a lifelike quality to what may seem strange, and they therefore engender interpersonal connections.

Data from empirical research and data from conflicting interpretations are critical to gaining insight into complicated environments. William James (1977) crystallized this need to integrate the dialectical opposites of the comprehensive and apprehensive—that is, logical and affective— in his scissors metaphor, "a man can no more limit himself to either [one] than a pair of scissors can cut with a single one of its blades" (p. 243). When the focus is on integrating the arguments with the stories, organizations increase their base of knowledge and their influence. Partially because Western organizational cultures tend to privilege and encourage the logical more than the imaginative, my emphasis here is on authenticating the valuable role of storytelling and narrative as a necessary complement, not as the only correct or true approach.

Wherein Lies the Truth?

The search for truth is an age-old philosophical conundrum. When trying to understand the human dimensions of organizational and group dynamics, a fundamental underlying assumption shaping a lot of organizational communication revolves around whether there is one truth, multiple legitimate interpretations, or both (McCall 1989; Stacey 2001). As Bruner says, "Arguments convince one of their truth, stories of their lifelikeness" (Bruner 1986, 11). The very nature of our perceptions about truth is in question.

When dualistic thinking and scientific method are privileged, the co-equal value of the affective dimensions of human behavior becomes obscured. Furthermore, when working with or in complex organizational settings, it is especially important to include narrative voices from diverse stakeholders who offer insight into how "events are seen through a particular set of personal prisms" (Bruner 1990, 54). Thus, neither one story nor a few stories provide a complete or reliable picture of organizational life.

I am reminded of a common saying in organizational folklore: *Perception is reality.* For instance, if workers perceive a manager as arrogant, the collective experience at least includes doubts about the manager regardless of her or his intentions or specific behavior. The workers' perceptions are part of the organizational life; the organizational reality.

Bruner (1990) invites us to "learn to distinguish, to use Yeats's phrase, 'the dancer from the dance.' A story is somebody's story" (p. 54). In other words, he suggests differentiating between a specific story told by one person and the collage of viable versions. Listening to multiple stories and perspectives paints a richer picture of the organizational milieu as in the earlier example of managers and workers. It also takes some time and commitment. The need to bring in these wide-ranging perspectives calls for the inclusion in the conversations of the less often heard voices and stories. These less familiar stories catalyze the collective understanding. Without them, the default modus operandi may be to rely on the seemingly quicker, easier route of focusing excessively on *a* story or the prevailing story. Because "stories are especially viable instruments for social negotiation" (Bruner 1990, 55), excluding divergent versions limits learning and silences voices. On the other hand, as people speak and know they are heard, as stories move across different contexts, relational bonds are deepened. Stories inform people's minds and touch their hearts.

The mutual construction of social, interpersonal truth is expressed by Palmer (1990): "truth [is] being involved in an eternal conversation about things that matter, conducted with passion and discipline. . . . truth is not in the conclusions so much as in the process of conversation itself" (p. 12). Like fitting new pieces into a large puzzle or transforming an artist's sketch into a painting, a range of stories bring in other parts, or a thicker description, of the whole (Geertz 1973), regardless of the power or status of the storyteller.

Trying to learn more about the sources of the perception is not the same thing as accepting or rejecting them as fact or truth. Instead, it is about gaining more insights to learn about the complex dynamics operating in the context. Often the nuanced perceptions below the surface are valuable clues that need to be heard to better understand the interpersonal whole. Gaining insight through hearing stories is similar to thickening the description to flesh out qualities of "lifelikeness" so that the unfamiliar becomes more accessible and alive. Renegotiating understanding involves hearing differing stories and remaining open to learning from them. Walker's metaphors about the texture of stories open the imagination into which participants can move to glean and negotiate more effective working relationships.

Culture as an Element of Truth

Interconnected stories and narrative accounts are always evolving within groups and organizations. The cultural heritages through which people develop their sense of morality, the worldviews through which people see life, and the paradigms that guide decision making are all overlapping, interwoven sets of stories. Stories about heroes and ideal leaders are examples. These recurring patterns of conversation are primary mediums for learning the moral codes of a culture and are mutually reinforcing as they are passed on over time. There are stories about people who are revered and others about individuals who should not be emulated. For example, the "can you believe he . . ." kinds of stories communicate indirectly, yet very clearly, behaviors that are considered inappropriate. Although the messages are often implicit, they become part of the social DNA.

To illustrate with a personal experience, when I was growing up in the southeastern United States, I was very close to my grandfather. I was often told stories about how he respected and honored everyone he met no matter their background, race, education, or income level. As far back as I can remember, I watched him to see what that kind of behavior would actually look like and how his behavior might differ from others. I unconsciously assessed the congruence between the stories and his actions. Over time, I internalized his values, although I have no memories of him explicitly speaking of them. Not until I was an adult did I realize how these stories about him and my subsequent ongoing observations shaped fundamental parts of my sense of morality.

These same dynamics occur at the organizational and societal level. The tone or themes of a culture's stories both reflect and shape it as they discourage counterculture behaviors. For instance, in some cultures people tell and repeat stories that bolster the importance of living in harmony with nature, the earth, and plant, animal, and human life. Their stories about the most respected people, stories about desirable family life, stories about preferred work life and community life carry themes that encourage people to respect nature and look to nature for guidance. The stories of many American Indians and First Nation peoples are il-

162 CATALYTIC CONVERSATIONS

lustrative. When harmony with nature is primary, renewal of the natural environment and of animal and fish populations is more likely to be an integral part of how people feed and support themselves. These cultural values and themes also influence human-made development patterns. The story lines of these cultures are incongruent with rationalizations for pollution or other short-term perspectives.

The stories of the dominant U.S. culture carry different prominent themes. They tend to communicate the invaluable rights of individual freedom and the responsibility of each person to work hard. Heroes in the cultures are more likely to be remembered for feats that protect freedom than efforts to protect nature. War stories communicate justifications of war for the sake of individual freedom. Thus, story lines emerge that are different from the stories of some American Indians or First Nation people.

Conversation and stories are a primary medium for creating and perpetuating *organizational* cultures as well. When you hear stories about highly regarded people in organizational settings that are familiar to you, what behaviors are mentioned? Are the long hours that people work promoted? Are their interpersonal skills admired? Are people who bring the most money into the organization praised highly? Are efforts to notice people's potential and to help them prepare themselves for roles with greater responsibility appreciated? Is efficiency held in high esteem? Are standards for high quality lauded? Through these stories, the norms for success, respect, and status are communicated. In the same way, stories about people who are not highly regarded provide counter images.

Clues to the prevailing values and priorities of organizational cultures are readily apparent through watching and listening to stories. This process is the essence of socialization. Cultures are protected, passed on to new arrivals, and reinforced through socialization, much of which is communicated through storytelling.

Through interlocking stories and themes, cultural values offer continuity and stability to organizational life. However, when changes are needed, the interlocking stories present formidable obstacles to change. The stories must shift for the culture to change, meaning that the nature of conversation also must make a transition. The most elemental aspect of the context is the nature of our conversations. By definition, catalytic conversations provoke change as people begin to see complexities and possibilities not imagined before, and new stories emerge.

Given the challenge that change presents, there are situations that call for organizations to move toward the most profound and challenging kind of learning, that of triple-loop learning (Isaacs 1993; Romme and van Witteloostruijn 1999). This kind of learning requires participants to actually turn to the nature of the context within which they are working and living to ask themselves what it is in the context that needs to change (Bateson 1972). They ask questions such as,

> What is leading me and others to have a predisposition to learning in this way at all? Why these goals? . . . Triple loop learning is the learning that opens inquiry into underlying 'whys.' It is the learning that permits insight into the nature of paradigm itself, not merely an assessment of which paradigm is superior. (Isaacs 1993, 30)

Group members thus question the habitual patterns that are holding them back from more constructive and generative behavior and transformative knowledge.

Tacit Knowledge That Can Seem out of Reach

Ironically, human behavior and organizational dynamics hold a myriad of bewildering mysteries. Let's explore another way to frame different ways of knowing. There are so many important things that are seemingly too difficult to understand. For instance,

- How does a manager know how to motivate an employee as she constructively and respectfully gives negative feedback?
- How does a mechanic know how to fix a machine by listening to it?
- How do flute makers know how to create instruments with a distinctive sound and feel?
- How does a musician playing by ear know how to create music?
- How does the skilled negotiator sense when it is time to wait and when it is time to intervene?
- How does a seasoned facilitator help a group of people collaborate in ways they never imagined they could?

In these examples, skill development is essential and specific kinds of knowledge are necessary. Yet much of the skill and knowledge is not readily accessible in ways that can be articulated, because it is tacit. It is essentially impossible to describe how a flute maker creates an instrument with an exquisite, unique tone. Playing music by ear is inexplicable to most people. An exquisite sense of timing in management and negotiation is artfully intuitive. Rarely do people learn these ways of knowing from a class or a book or in a training program where explicit knowledge is the standard. A seemingly circuitous route is needed to extend tacit expertise and knowing throughout organizations, and the process can seem costly and illusive.

Even in the more recent Western literature, there is still a "tendency to treat knowledge as being essentially of one kind. . . . to privilege the individual over the group, and the explicit over the tacit (as if . . . [they] were two variations of one knowledge, not separate distinct forms of knowledge)" (Cook and Brown 1999, 382). A major challenge for contemporary organizations is to tap a full range of the tacit and explicit knowledge of individuals and groups. Story and narrative act in concert to make multiple kinds of knowledge more accessible.

A wealth of research has emerged in recent decades from an unlikely combination of disciplines. The work that is especially relevant to this book is generally found under the rubrics of organizational learning, knowledge management, and entrepreneurialism. Yet, even these areas have become so diverse that they include research from across management, highly technical information systems spheres, the physical sciences, and organizational behavior, for example.

Although there are many ways to conceptualize different ways of knowing, the tacit and explicit knowledge of individuals and groups are particularly pertinent (see Figure 9.2). Polanyi's (1983) work differentiating tacit and explicit knowledge is an important foundation for much of the recent research in organizational studies, quantum physics, and experiential learning. Understanding the interplay between what individuals and organizations learn is closely related.

Organizations are not single entities that learn. Instead, individuals have both tacit and explicit knowledge, tacit and explicit ways of learning, and preferences for how they learn. The challenge is how to bring the individual and tacit knowledge into communal space to catalyze learning, adaptation, innovation, and regenerative change for groups within the organization and the organization as a whole

Let's look at the meaning of *tacit, explicit,* and *implicit knowing.* The most commonly used description to distinguish between tacit and explicit knowledge originated with Polanyi's (1983) example of knowing how to ride a bicycle, which calls upon both kinds of knowing. Explicit knowledge includes things that we know and can describe to another

Figure 9.2 **Four ways of knowing and storytelling as a medium for learning**

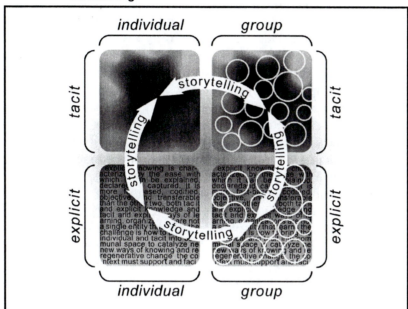

person; for example, how to place your feet on the pedals as you begin and how to stop the bicycle. On the other hand, it is difficult to put into words how to balance yourself well enough not to fall down (i.e., the tacit knowledge). Although people can talk about getting a *feel* for the bicycle, the person learning to ride must learn that *feeling* for herself/ himself by actually riding and experiencing it. Riding a bicycle, like many other things, depends on having both kinds of knowledge.

Sharing tacit experiences and collectively creating new ways of knowing "depends on being in a world that is inseparable from our bodies, our language, and our social history" (Varela et al. 1992, 149). Embodied experiences are also at the core of the nature of learning as articulated in the work of William James (1890) and John Dewey (1997). They both recognized the inseparable nature of learning and experience, i.e., the essence of experiential learning, which incorporates experience into the cognitive transmission of explicit knowledge. Conversations, stories, and narrative accounts are mediums through which these kinds of embodied reflections unfold communally (Baker, Jensen, and Kolb 2002; Boje 1991; Bruner 1990; Callahan and Elliott 1996).

Explicit knowing, which is easily articulated, is a polar opposite of the tacit, which is difficult or impossible to put into words. Explicit knowing tends to be more fact-based, codified, objective, and transferable than implicit and tacit forms. Relatively easy to explain, declare, and capture, examples of explicit knowledge include a set of procedures, an instruction manual for a computer training program, or a report of a randomized empirical study.

Implicit knowing is similar in that it can be verbalized, although it is not codified in any given context. There may be hints about such knowledge or it may be implied, but it has not yet been fully explicated. For instance, implicit knowledge might be the knowledge gained through personal observation of interactions among people who make up the social networks within an organization: who knows whom, who has access to whom, or who has influence. By observing and paying attention, an employee or client can get a sense of how to do their work through these networks and gradually learn about the organization. People often develop implicit understandings about an organization, even if unconsciously, before actually being able to put them into words.

Tacit knowing is even more ephemeral and remains inarticulate. It develops out of practice and experience at work and in life. Craftspeople who make leather saddles that mold themselves to the riders learn their craft through years of observing, apprenticeship, trial, and error; they learn through practice.

Embedded in the social, collective environments of intertwined relationships is the recursive movement of tacit, implicit, and explicit ways of knowing and knowledge. People create and continuously renew their knowledge through iterative, recursive processes (Griffith, Sawyer, and Neale 2003; Nonaka 1994). Figure 9.3 illustrates the notion that recursivity is not linear or sequential.

Knowing does not have to be implicit before moving from the tacit to explicit or the reverse though the knowing often does become implicit. For example, as the explicit aspects of a person's work become more and more familiar over time, they frequently take on an implicit quality before the worker thoroughly internalizes them as tacit knowledge—e.g., "It is second nature to me now." Or a person's tacit knowing can become explicit in a burst of realization to others as they learn through collective reflections, dialogue, and storytelling in response to a challenge; when a few experienced people tell stories that reveal their deeply embedded

Figure 9.3 **The recursive flow of the tacit, implicit, and explicit**

tacit understanding of the interconnections among the organization's stakeholders, for example. The stories and comments illustrate to the less experienced group members how vital it is to know and understand each other well, as it leads to learning through relationships and conversations. Broad, abstract statements about dense social networks become concrete and immediate as new members listen to the more seasoned.

In other words, knowledge is "usable" when a team not only has the explicit knowledge to accomplish its work but also has "the necessary tacit knowledge, both at the individual and social level, to know when and how to use that knowledge" (Griffith, et al. 2003, 269–270). Nonaka (1994) describes this dynamic process as "a continual dialogue between explicit and tacit knowledge" (p. 15) in his classic article creating a conceptual framework for understanding organizational knowledge creation.

Problem-solving knowledge likewise is harder to transfer from one person to another because it "tends to have more tacit components" (Griffith et al. 2003, 270). Tacit knowing is difficult to explain or describe because the knowing is gained over time and becomes so much a part of the learners that it is almost as though it is incorporated into the very cells of their bodies.

Figure 9.4 **Unleashing collective, collaborative wisdom**

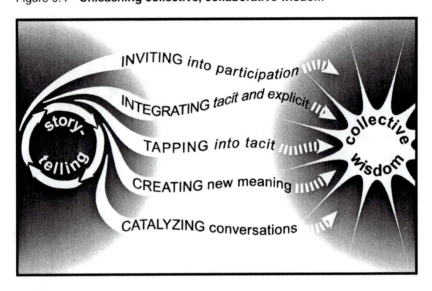

> [S]haring "knowing how" can be seen as a process of enabling others to learn the practice that entails the "knowing how." It is a process of helping others develop the ability to enact—in a variety of contexts and conditions—the knowing in practice. (Orlikowski 2002, 271)

Because it is fundamental to sustaining and improving quality, organizations need to find ways to help support the sharing of "know-how."

Bringing Tacit Knowledge into the Collective Environment

To bring out the tacit and explicit knowledge embedded in a group or organization, it is important to build a context that facilitates *shared interpretation* so that people can develop collective wisdom. To grasp and articulate this *collaborative wisdom,* I suggest there are at least four ongoing cultural norms that benefit organizations (see Figure 9.4). Although not definitive, these norms include the following:

- Inviting
- Tapping
- Integrating
- Creating

Inviting

Sharing stories typically attracts attention more easily than didactic statements. By listening to the experiences of others, "our personal experience mingles with what we hear and then see . . . we fill in the blanks and gaps between the lines with our own experiences in response to the cues . . . the audible story is only a fraction of the connection between people" (Boje 1991, 107). Stories bring into play the *pull* mode as distinct from pushing or trying to force others into engagement. Stories invite people into participation, rather than trying to push them into prescribed behavior.

Part of the invitation is in the texture of a story. As Walker (1998) described, stories are *elastic like gauze* rather than hard and rigid. Unlike the tight consistency of didactic monologues, the texture of stories is loose enough to invite the experiences of others.

Let me share an example to illustrate. Once I was working with a group in an organization that had to make substantial changes because of new demands from the external environment. One person spoke passionately about past events in the organization to make a case for why he was sure that changes were impossible. The former leader had initiated a major change effort that failed miserably and resulted in major layoffs. The speaker's fear was palpable. Rather than try to argue or give rational reasons about how this situation was different, I shared a recollection from another organization that had successfully faced a similar challenge. I was careful not to editorialize with my conclusions about the meaning of the story. Instead, I told it briefly and then remained quiet to let the group respond. I carefully facilitated in a low-key manner as they talked.

Although the conversation that followed was not concise or linear, I did keep the group on topic. Gradually, people began to figure out how they might meet their challenges and move forward constructively. My story helped shift the conversation away from whether they could change or not. With a little guidance, they developed ways to meet the problems rather than having me impose my way upon them. By being invited into the process, the group developed their own alternatives to which they, in turn, felt committed instead of dismissing or resisting externally imposed directives.

The texture of stories also allows people to relate to multiple facets of their lives, that is, personal and professional. The work is more inviting when they can do as Boje (1991) suggests: "fill in the blanks and gaps between the lines with [their] own experiences." For example, when I work with people to help them develop constructive conflict negotiation skills, the explicit purpose is to improve their ability to be more effective in their organizational lives. Yet in most groups, people recognize and mention openly to the group or to me later that these skills are relevant in their personal lives as well. They see that developing conflict negotiation skills can also affect their roles as parents, as grown children relating to their parents, as spouses or partners, as friends, as members of religious communities, and as community activists to name a few. Even though they do not share details of these connections, they fill in the blanks for themselves.

Tapping

Rather than fixed and tangible, much of the complexity of human behavior and organizational life operates in the realms of tacitness, know-how, intuition, and unconscious feelings and assumptions. Stories increase awareness more readily than the linearity of causal logic because they tap into intuitive or tacit capacities and memories.

To illustrate, I draw on an ethnographic study involving several people trying to repair a critical machine in a large corporation (Brown and Duguid 1991; Orr 1990). Near the end of this chapter, I compare this process in a manufacturing facility to a consulting case in which I was asked to try to repair broken relationships. In both situations, the substantive work was among the people involved, yet the results were different. The machine repair was definitive; the result was a working machine. When the repairs are interpersonal and relational, however, results are far more ambiguous.

In the corporation, the situation involved a service technician (referred to as a rep) and a technical specialist faced with a malfunctioning machine giving copious error codes that did not tally with the ways that it crashed when tested. This case is an example of the kind of serious problems that workers have to solve when situations do not match any of the procedures or decision trees in repair manuals for "what to do when." It is a common gap between documented, codified knowledge of an organization and the actual practices of everyday work. In other words, what does a worker do when faced with the erratic functions of a machine that do not fit into any of the conditions covered in the training programs and repair manuals, which represent the explicit, codified knowledge?

When unable to repair the machine, the rep first followed procedures of the corporation by asking for assistance from the specialist, a highly experienced supervisor whose job included troubleshooting such problems. The specialist was also unable to figure out the problem. The interpersonal dynamics between the two people are also relevant. The rep was more experienced with less formal education, while the specialist was younger and had more academic status. Thus, their collaboration was also part of the work. After considerable effort and no success, the two people were faced with the dilemma of whether to resort to replacing the expensive equipment. This alternative represented a defeat on multiple levels, including high financial cost to the corporation and loss of legitimacy for both workers with their customer, their colleagues, and the corporation.

Trying to avoid these unhappy consequences, they engaged in a day-long effort and about five continuous hours of intense interaction. During that time, they shared and compared their experiences when faced with previous malfunctions with this machine and similar equipment as well as what they knew from experiences they had heard about (i.e., a long series of stories) (Orr 1990). Because the problem they faced did not fit any of the common patterns from the codified knowledge or the previous experiences of either of them, they were unable to depend on explicit organizational knowledge or individual tacit knowledge to repair it. Having tapped into their stories of previous experiences, they were faced with a need to integrate them in new ways.

Integrating

Tacit knowledge comes to the surface as old-timers in an organization tell stories about crises and how they worked through them. If that is as far as the conversations go, however, and the newcomers and less experienced employees do not stay in conversation with the more experienced workers over time or bring what they hear into their practices, learning is not likely to become collective. The potential use of the old-timers' tacit knowledge to facilitate learning and adaptation to changing environments is limited. It must first be integrated into and become a part of the "here and now" demands of the organization.

By returning to the example of the rep and specialist, the importance of integration becomes more clear. Previous problems with this machine were not solved, and much of the data the machine gave had not made sense to any of the reps or specialists who had tried to decipher it. As the rep and specialist worked together, engaging in a long, arduous back-and-forth process, their "stories generated sufficient interplay among memories, tests, the machine's responses, and the ensuing insights to lead to diagnosis and repair. . . . these separate experiences converged, leading to a shared diagnosis of certain previously encountered but unresolved symptoms . . . [and they] constructed a communal interpretation of hitherto uninterpretable data and individual experience" (Brown and Duguid 1991, 44). The two people each brought unique and overlapping expertise and experience to the problem. They engaged in what I would call catalytic conversations (per Figure 9.4) as they worked together to diagnose the cause of the problem and then to repair the broken machine. While the specialist had more formal education and training, the rep had worked on these machines for a longer period of time. Together, they gradually became more explicit with each other and integrated what they knew, observed, and heard into a new understanding to overcome this challenging problem. Together they literally created new knowledge and new understanding, which neither of the individuals had previously.

Without the transformative qualities of the integration of multiple ways of knowing and committed interpersonal efforts to share and integrate expertise, the potential for problem solving and for innovation is undermined. In addition to inviting, tapping, and integrating differing kinds of knowledge, a further challenge is to change the practices of work so it can be used to create new ways of working.

Creating

It is in the bringing together and integrating of the tacit, implicit, explicit, individual, and group knowledge that the fusion of horizons is possible (Gadamer 1994). By *fusion* Gadamer does not mean that an individual or one kind of knowledge is subsumed by another. On the contrary, he describes how people collaboratively create new knowledge, understanding, and practices that no one individual or group could have accomplished alone; he recognizes the relational, communal qualities of collaboration. Through an authentic openness to questioning, people "bring out the undetermined possibilities" (Gadamer 1994, 375).

It is also in the collective inviting, tapping, and integrating of the less accessible ways of knowing that the likelihood for problem solving and innovation is increased. These three precursors provide the necessary foundation to increase an organization's capacity to do what I refer to as unleashing resources that are hard to reach, taking the next step toward creating something new.

The meaning of events unfolds through people's conversations, experiences, reflections, and narrative accounts as they make sense of what they face and the world around them. In the story of the rep and specialist who figured out together how to repair the erratic machine, they solved the irascible problem and created new knowledge in a particular context. In the following weeks and months, especially in the company cafeteria, this story was told over and over among employees as it passed into the communal know-how of the corporation. This case is an excellent demonstration of how two individuals used storytelling to tap and integrate their tacit knowledge and fill in the gaps between the codified, explicit group knowledge and the serious problem they faced. Then, through the telling and retelling of the story throughout the organization, this tacit knowledge was brought into the communal space of the corporation as a source of ongoing learning at the collective level for others. Moreover, it provided a model of how such interactions can advance personal and organizational goals.

The way people make sense of their environment, the meaning they create, is never static. They negotiate and renegotiate meanings over time as new problems and unexpected situations arise. New people and fresh ideas come into play, and demands and constraints change. Sense making materializes in a particular context as the people involved in that time and place make it. It does not transport exactly from one context to another. There is a fine line between ongoing renegotiation of meaning and the meaning specific to one context. "Stories and their telling can reflect the complex social web within which work takes place . . . The stories have a flexible generality that makes them both adaptable and particular. They function, rather like the common law, as a usefully under-constrained means to interpret each new situation in the light of accumulated wisdom and constantly changing circumstances" (Brown and Duguid 1991, 44–45).

In these ways, the mediums of narrative accounts and storytelling are more fluid and less controlling than didactic language. The meaning and interpretations that listeners make from stories is more malleable as they make sense and give shape to what they hear. As meaning is renegotiated collectively with others through stories, expertise and ideas more easily cross from one context to another as people adapt practices, integrate them into new contexts, and create new meanings. As Boje (1991) says, "our personal experience mingles with what we hear and then see. As listeners, we are coproducers with the teller of the story" (p. 107). Creativity thrives more readily in fluid, malleable conversations though it often does not happen without intentional efforts and boundaries.

Building Shared Interpretation

> For it is not shared stories or shared information so much as shared interpretation that binds people together . . . Learning to tell their . . . stories . . . allowed all to share in their major resource—their collective, collaborative wisdom. (Brown and Duguid 2000, 107)

Proactively creating organizational environments that support storytelling involves the kinds of norms I describe earlier, people learning more about how to tell stories, and a blend of giving space while also clearly articulating boundaries and expectations about results.

Storytelling is a kind of conversation that comes more naturally to some people than to others, although participating as a speaker or listener is a learnable talent even when it is not intuitive. Keeping the story concise and ensuring that it is appropriate for the context in which it will be told are key markers of good storytelling. Weaving the story into the conversation or selecting a cogent part of a story heightens the effectiveness.

In another example, these principles of storytelling were used with only partial success. I worked with an intact group of about ten people to overcome a crisis and to help them identify the underlying source of their extremely serious animosity and ongoing interpersonal problems. I asked and received the go-ahead to bring in a co-facilitator. My co-facilitator and I each had considerable tacit and explicit knowledge about organizational and group dynamics and about this specific group and the environment within which they worked. In addition, we each brought specific experiences that complemented the other. To draw our tacit knowledge to the surface for the benefit of the project, however, my co-facilitator and I had to converse and share stories with each other about similar situations we had experienced. In our conversations, we could clarify ways that this group was and was not comparable to others in our experiences. We asked each other many questions, thus pulling out even more of our intuitive ways of knowing.

As we began the work, the director told the group we would work with them, and we had an opening meeting. In retrospect, I think we could have done a better job of inviting the group members into the process. They received what they probably perceived as a directive from their leader to cooperate, and the tension was so high that they felt compelled to participate. Beginning the process differently would not have been easy, but the benefit may have been worth the effort.

Within a few weeks, either my co-facilitator or I had interviewed each person individually, asking semistructured questions to invite them to share their experiences through examples, most of which came out in the forms of stories. In some cases we also met with parts of the group together, and we began a series of whole-group meetings that we co-facilitated.

To prepare for the group sessions, my co-facilitator and I shared information and stories that we had heard in our individual meetings and talked about our interpretations. We tried together to understand the deeply embroiled turf battles, tensions, and complexities of the situation among these high-achieving professionals, many of whom had larger-than-life egos. Our norms of tapping and trying to integrate our varied ways of knowing were paramount. We created meeting agendas with clear structures while also providing time to draw people out to talk about their perceptions of problems. After group meetings, the two of us privately debriefed by talking at length about what had happened and again sharing our interpretations.

My co-facilitator and I had differing interpretations at times. Talking through our differences led us to try to recall specific data to support them, to question our assumptions, and to understand the situation at a far deeper level than I could have done alone. In other words, we often had catalytic conversations that inspired us to see things in novel ways, to consider them in a new light, and talk about unanticipated alternatives. Sometimes these conversations were lengthy and would spill over into subsequent meetings with each other. Over time, we were able to agree on most of our interpretations while also striving to leave ourselves open for new data to alter our perceptions.

We gradually shared our interpretations with the group and asked for their responses and suggestions. Although it took numerous sessions and considerable angst, we were able to reach consensus with the group about many, yet not all, of the underlying causes of their chronic difficulties. Group members gained new insight, but they were unwilling to face the primary dilemmas with their authoritarian leader.

Unlike the earlier example, we were not working with a machine, although the crux of the problem solving in both situations involved people and their relationships and perceptions. However, we could not ultimately turn a machine on to see if it would run and continue working. It was not ever possible to conclude exactly which interpretations were the correct or the *true* ones. This case is a good illustration of how there is rarely an absolute truth when working with human interactions.

When I reflect on the outcomes of the work, I could interpret the group as one that was not sufficiently ready to change. I could say it was a group not ready to accept some of our interpretations, or that we were unable to articulate adequately some of the complexities operating in their environment. There were power inequities that participants were unwilling to challenge, even though we tried; and they were under severe work and time pressures that prevented them from remaining engaged in our work long enough to make significant changes. In retrospect, I think there are elements of *truth* in all of these interpretations. Although the group began to create new ways of collective understanding, I do not think it ever made the necessary changes to develop collective wisdom. I realize, in retrospect, that if we had asked them to retell some of their stories in the group, the retelling might have been a useful way to tap into their potential for understanding more from others' perspectives and renewing their damaged relationships.

Sharing this story of a less than satisfactory ending is not entirely easy. Yet it represents the challenges facing organizations and groups with strong differences of perspective in the workplace.

Conclusions

Perhaps the most valuable contribution of storytelling for organizations is the transformation of individual tacit knowledge as it interacts with the tacit knowledge of others and enters a collective reservoir for creating explicit new understanding and new knowledge. In other words, at this nexus people can move beyond transferring existing knowledge and know-how into more creative realms that facilitate collective innovation.

To unleash the knowing that is latent in organizational life, the full range of the tacit and explicit knowledge of individuals and groups must be easily accessible through conversations and operating in concert with each other. It is in the interface between having knowledge and knowing how to do something with it that the most exquisite creativity emerges. It is in the interface between what individuals know and what groups can collaboratively create together that innovation occurs in complex environments. Regenerative change depends on a rich integration of all of these resources.

References

Baker, A. C., P. Jensen, and D. Kolb. 2002. *Conversational learning: An experiential approach to knowledge creation.* Westport, CT: Quorum Books.

Bateson, G. 1972. *Steps to an ecology of the mind.* New York: Ballantine Books.

Boje, D. M. 1991. The storytelling organization: A study of story performance in an office-supply firm. *Administrative Science Quarterly* 36: 106–126.

Brown, J. S., and P. Duguid. 1991. Organizational learning and communities-of-practice: Toward a unified view of working, learning and innovation. *Organization Science* 2 (1): 40–57.

———. 2000. *The social life of organization.* Boston: Harvard Business School Press.

Brown, J. S., S. Denning, K. Groh, and L. Prusak. 2004. *Storytelling in organizations: Why storytelling is transforming 21st century organizations and management.* Burlington, MA: Elsevier Butterworth-Heinemann.

Bruner, J. 1986. *Actual minds, possible worlds.* Cambridge, MA: Harvard University Press.

———. 1990. *Acts of meaning.* Cambridge, MA: Harvard University Press.

Callahan, C., and C. S. Elliott. 1996. Listening: A narrative approach to everyday understandings and behavior. *Journal of Economic Psychology* 17: 79–114.

Cook, S D. N., and J. S. Brown. 1999. Bridging epistemologies: The generative dance between organizational knowledge and organizational knowing. *Organizational Science* 10 (4): 381–400.

Dewey, J. 1997. *Experience and education.* New York: Touchstone. (Orig. pub. 1938.)

Gadamer, H. G. 1994. *Truth and method.* 2d rev. ed. New York: Crossroad. (Orig. pub. 1989).

Geertz, C. 1973. *The interpretation of cultures.* New York: Basic Books.

Griffith, T. L., J. E. Sawyer, and M. A. Neale. 2003. Virtualness and knowledge in teams: Managing the love triangle of organizations, individuals, and information technology. *MIS Quarterly* 27 (2): 265–287.

Isaacs, W. 1993. Taking flight: Dialogue, collective thinking, and organizational learning. *Organizational Dynamics* 22 (2):24–39.

James, W. 1977. Percept and concept: The import of concepts. In *The writings of William James,* ed. J. McDermott. Chicago: University of Chicago Press.

———. 2007. *The principles of psychology.* New York: Holt, Rinehart and Winston. (Orig. pub. 1890.)

Kolb, D. A. 1984. *Experiential learning: Experience as the source of learning and development.* Englewood Cliffs, NJ: Prentice-Hall.

McCall, M. M. 1989. The significance of storytelling. *Imprint* 5: 39–47.

Nonaka, I. 1994. A dynamic theory of organizational knowledge creation. *Organization Science* 5 (1): 14–37.

Orlikowski, W. J. 2002. Knowing in practice: Enacting a collective capability in distributed organizing. *Organization Science* 13 (3): 249–273.

Orr, J. 1990. Sharing knowledge, celebrating identity: War stories and community memory in a service culture. In *Collective remembering: Memory in a service culture,* ed. D. Middleton and D. Edwards. Beverly Hills, CA: Sage.

Palmer, P. 1990. Good teaching: A matter of living the mystery. *Change* 22 (1): 11–16.

Polanyi, M. 1983. *The tacit dimension.* Gloucester, MA: Peter Smith.

Romme, G. L., and A. van Witteloostruijn. 1999. Circular organizing and triple loop learning. *Journal of Organizational Change Management* 12 (5): 439–453.

Stacey, R. D. 2001. *Complex responsive processes in organizations,* New York: Routledge.

Tulving, E. 1983. *Elements of episodic memory.* New York: Oxford University Press.

Van Maanen, J. 1995. Style as theory. *Organization Science* 6 (1): 133–143.

Varela, Francisco J., Evan Thompson, and Eleanor Rosch. 1992. *The embodied mind: Cognitive science and human experience.* Boston: MIT Press.

Vitz, P. C. 1990. The use of stories in moral development: New psychological reasons for an old education method. *American Psychologist* 45 (6): 709–720.

Walker, A. 1998. *By the light of my father's smile.* New York: Ballantine Books.

Wenger, E. 1998. *Communities of practice: Learning, meaning, and identity.* New York: Cambridge University Press.

Part III

10

The Dynamics of Organizational Change and Innovation

This book is grounded in empirical and theoretical research, case studies, and wide-ranging practitioner experience, as well as in my intuition. The book's overarching message, contrary to prevailing perspectives, is the value of differences among stakeholders as potential resources for generative change, knowledge creation, and innovation.

The approach developed involves a fundamentally new way of thinking about organizational life that recognizes conversational interactions as the medium through which work, communication, and innovation occur. When people embrace catalytic conversations in an intentionally created environment of authentic respect and the full engagement of differences, new potential is unleashed. The differences too often avoided or fought against become catalysts for innovation. As participants integrate their multiple interpretations to discover new knowledge together, they engage in conversational learning and thus facilitate ongoing catalytic conversations and continuous learning (Baker, Jensen, and Kolb 2002). In this book, I distinguish the ingredients of this approach to enable organizations to intentionally foster catalytic conversations and innovation.

Differences in perspective, experience, priorities, values, education, background, and culture are increasingly a factor in workplaces and society and will only continue to expand. As seen in the controversial coastal land development case in Chapter 3, the stakeholders represented dramatically differing perspectives in spite of their shared interest in the economic well-being of the community in question. This book speaks directly to how people choose to deal with such differences and how to encourage workable and emergent interaction patterns.

My focus is on the infinitely renewable resources of conversational interactions and differences among people. Conversations are inroads to influencing change across the micro dimensions of human communication and the macro institutional structures of organizations and societies. These dynamics are mutually reinforcing as the micro and macro partially shape each other. In other words, interpersonal interactions among people at the micro level (e.g., who talks to whom and how freely or structured, who has input into decision making) collectively have powerful influences on the macrolevel structures of organizations. Simultaneously, the institutionalized structures of the organization—e.g., policies, hierarchy, or lack thereof—influence and partially shape interpersonal communication patterns.

A fundamental premise of the book is that people socially construct organizational dynamics, as their experiences and expectations lead to highly varied interpretations. These varied interpretations appear in organizational communication as differences. Catalytic conversations offer organizations constructive mediums into which differences can be channeled to become valuable resources for innovation (Bijlsma-Frankema, Rosendaal, and Taminiau 2006). Yet differences and human behavior can be volatile, requiring a high degree of intentionality to function as resources. While organizations cannot make people behave in reliably predictable ways, they can create enabling conditions that support knowledge creation and innovation (Nonaka 1994).

Catalytic conversations are not second nature for most people or the result of easy, linear, cause-and-effect interactions. Although linear causality never applied reasonably to human behavior, its lack of relevance is increasingly apparent in the contemporary world of global economies, changing technologies, and knowledge work. One of the current dilemmas is that, having departed the world of linear approximation, people are now "navigating on a very broad ocean" (Cowan in Waldrop, 1992; 66) of uncertainty.

In post-industrialized economies, most people no longer produce simple products via simple processes, such as making toys on a production line. The nature of work in these countries has changed. As Rycroft and Kash (1999) describe, work for many people now involves complex products and services via complex processes, or *knowledge work*. Thus, workers are more interdependent, relying on each other to access needed expertise, because no one person can fully know or understand such complexity. These changes make it more critical than ever for people to be able to work collaboratively with others and to be able to engage their differences constructively to share and create new knowledge.

Another primary premise of this book is that organizational strength and stakeholder vitality are not in conflict with each other. Regardless of whether organizations operate in for-profit, not-for-profit, or public arenas, they benefit dramatically when they can readily tap their stakeholders' expertise and energy in highly stimulating and supportive work environments. As demographics change in countries such as the United States, where there is an expectation of a large number of retirees in the next few decades and where workers are more and more diverse, organizations that are dependent on status quo modalities are exceedingly vulnerable. They must find ways to retain the organizational expertise, history, and knowledge of their retirees. They must intentionally anticipate the kinds of work environments that knowledge-workers in rapidly changing, ambiguous global economies need. One vital dimension of these work environments involves support for organizational communication that promotes catalytic conversations, knowledge creation, and innovation. Thus, intentionally attending to the contexts within which all stakeholders work and communicate offers immense positive potential to strengthen organizational well-being.

Implications for Organizations

This book builds on recent research that recognizes conversation as the medium through which the work of organizational life flows. The book goes beyond this concept to demonstrate the importance of integrating, not diminishing, the integrity of differing perspectives and interpretations. It establishes the value of catalytic conversations, listening for substantive change, constructive controversy, knowledge creation, ground-breaking innovation, and ways to encourage them. Whether focusing on economic viability, environmental well-being, or equity among people, the dynamics of a rapidly changing world press upon us to be more assertive and knowledgeable about how we want to move forward intentionally.

Enabling Contexts

Given the complexity of changing work patterns and human interactions, traditional managerial models that grew out of the industrial revolution are exceedingly outdated and must evolve and change dramatically.

These models impede organizational capacity to capitalize on rapidly changing environments and unexpected opportunities. They stifle people, flexibility, learning, and innovation. Moreover, the younger workers who are now replacing baby boomers, as in the United States, expect and demand qualitatively different working conditions.

When organizational contexts support fundamentally new communication patterns that embrace catalytic conversations, conversational learning, and constructive controversy, they also encourage the adaptation, flexibility, and spontaneity on which new economies depend. One challenge is to shift away from an orientation of *making* things happen toward an emphasis on fostering contexts that support more creative and humane behavior, that is, to shift away from designing the environment toward designing *for* the environment (Jacobs and Heracleous 2005).

What are the ingredients of designing *for* organizational contexts? One of the few absolute requirements is that mutual respect must be a prevailing norm. It is not an exaggeration to say that without respect, the idea of exploring differences, sharing knowledge, and creating emergent environments is not viable. Not only is respect a pragmatic requirement—people who are respected resist less and respond more positively—but it is also the bedrock of professionalism and integrity.

A second and closely related characteristic of designing *for* an organization is to foster generative change through trusting relationships among stakeholders. Generally, it is not possible for people to enter the uncharted territory of risks taking and thinking beyond the boundaries of convention if they cannot trust their fellow workers to not embarrass or humiliate them. They need to feel confident that their unintentional mistakes and failures will not be used against them; trust and psychological safety must be in place (Edmondson 2003). As has been shown previously, ample research supports the assumption that groups and teams with trusting relationships in which members feel psychologically safe learn more, learn faster, and perform better. Moreover, communication based on these enriching qualities promotes risk taking, questioning, and vulnerability that are precursors to knowledge creation and innovation.

Likewise, in the dynamic interactions of generative change, the potential for self-development and innovation is vast. As organizations experience the overlapping pressures of changing technologies, increasing diversity, and more complexity, they and their stakeholders must have "an ability to self-organize and regenerate [themselves] on a continuous basis" (Morgan 2006, 97). In other words, the work contexts must be less hierarchical and more flexible. They must allow the spontaneity associated with the passionate pursuit of quality, ideas, and new possibilities. The work environment must facilitate identifying and working with other people who share similar interests and have the necessary complementary expertise because micromanagement and inflexible hierarchical chains of command suppress energy and stifle creativity. Accountability for high quality work is not sacrificed. Instead, the work environment and parameters within which work is accomplished change.

A third aspect of context, as described in Chapter 3, is to make it possible for people to have opportunities to work together at the edge of chaos where emergence thrives. Stakeholders involved in dense web-like communication networks and self-organizing behaviors can access expertise as needed and be especially creative. Yet if we look at the continuum between order and chaos, there is a natural tendency for people to constantly reorder themselves, becoming more structured and more ordered. When trying to work at the edge of chaos, the only way to avoid retreating into the familiarity of order and stability or slipping into chaos is through deliberate *intentionality*. When people can move in the direction of chaos without slipping over into it, the edge of chaos is an incredibly creative environment. When organizations allow people to be spontaneous, share responsibility, be flexible enough to go off-line to talk about new approaches, and to follow their passion and curiosity for higher quality work, the stage is primed for emergence at the edge of chaos.

The fourth ingredient needed to successfully design *for* organizations is congruence. Well-known markers of congruence are *walking the talk* and *talking the walk*. When spoken messages are in line with behavior, authenticity is apparent. People sense the authenticity. Even when people do not utter the words *congruence* and *authenticity* the groundwork for a relationship of trust begins to take hold in the presence of congruence.

The phenomenon of congruence is vital both within a person and within an organization. For example, if I sense authenticity and congruence in a colleague, it is easier for me to be open and begin to reveal small vulnerabilities to test it. If I sense authenticity and congruence in my organization I find it energizing, and I am more likely to develop commitment and loyalty. Although absolutely consistent congruence is extremely challenging, the cumulative potential of escalating relationships of trust built on congruence and authenticity is expansive and can become mutually reinforcing dynamics that support generative change among people in an organization.

The fifth ingredient is reflection. Often, reflection in Western organizational settings is perceived as wasting time. Yet the kinds of interactions and learning required for knowledge creation and innovation are minimized without reflection upon experiences and practices. By blending engagement with reflection, a person or a group can more readily learn from mistakes and imagine alternatives and new possibilities that were unlikely without reflection (see Chapter 8).

As with congruence, reflection has both individual and collective dimensions. This book focuses primarily on the collective because of its relevance to catalytic conversations, knowledge creation, and innovation at the group, organizational, and interorganizational levels. When people collectively reflect upon shared experiences in a context of generative change, once again the potential for relationship building, continuous learning, and creative behavior expands. As participants try to figure out how their best work occurs and how they can alter their less productive engagements, they allow the *situations to talk back* to them (Schon 1983). In other words, they learn what their work situation is telling them. They gather new data. For example, when the situation, or setting, demonstrates resistance, it provides new information such as a lack of readiness or a lack of training for impending change. Ignoring widespread resistance is not wise or efficient. Having open conversations and exploring the sources of the resistance can save enormous amounts of time in the long run. These new sources of data function as differences that begin to stimulate consideration of unanticipated concerns and catalyze new understandings.

The sixth ingredient is to foster the substantive conversations that provide a tether between the parts of the past that participants do not want to lose and the future that they want to create. For example, an organization may have a reputation and sense of history that it does not want to jeopardize. At the same time, the organization may very much want to take advantage of a completely new market if it is a business, or tackle a challenging new policy issue in the public sector. A key to catalytic conversations and innovation is to bring relevant underlying assumptions to the surface and deliberately engage stakeholders in conversations about germane issues. In such conversations, participants can honor the fundamental values of the past while exploring new directions. By bringing these relevant considerations to the surface in the conversations, unconscious, unexamined assumptions are much less likely to blindly impede the organization's adaptability.

Participants must tailor these processes to each context based on the time frame of the opportunity and the organization's capacity for and experience with using catalytic conversations and conversational learning processes. However, while situations vary widely, in catalytic conversations the principles of honoring the most important historical elements are considered in light of needs and opportunities to move in new, innovative directions. Thus, as people make changes in light of the past and the future they want to create, they do not simply bounce from one fad to another; nor do they blindly resist change. They do not change for the sake of change or for the sake of taking action. By looking back and seeing ahead, they *intentionally incorporate the past that they want to bring forward into the future they want to create.*

Developing Competency

To engage constructively in these enabling environments, participants also need to develop the competencies and skills that facilitate their capacity to function well and rise to the higher purposes of their work. They need to know how to work together in a mode of inquiry that looks at differing points of view from a variety of vantage points while not losing sight of the importance of decisiveness and productivity. Many of the skills described below support ongoing inquiry, such as asking open-ended questions and listening for new insight and surprise.

People must learn how to work and live in ambiguous and unpredictable settings and accept the dynamics of ongoing change. If people are too uncomfortable with ambiguity, the tendency is to try to order the environment in ways that undermine the self-organizing and emergent behaviors at the core of continuous learning and innovation. Further complicating these dynamics are the macro forces of change that cannot be stopped. Thus, efforts to stop the change are likely to be unsuccessful while, ironically, these efforts may also obstruct the positive dynamics usually associated with ambiguity, such as spontaneity, flexibility, and adaptability.

Another competency is for participants to learn how to see beyond the easy, short-term interventions intended to fix problems. Instead, the focus needs to be broader and more long term, considering implications and consequences. This new perspective also allows people to shift the responsibility for change and decision making away from one or just a few people. Seeking wide, diverse input early in projects and on an ongoing basis denotes a prevailing norm of inclusiveness and a distributed responsibility across multiple populations of participants. At the same time, inclusiveness and distributed responsibility does not preclude the need for decisiveness and boundaries.

For example, in Chapter 6, I described the CEO who embarked on a major change effort and initially sought input from many people. He abandoned inclusive participation when he grew impatient and began to prescribe the changes he wanted. When he ended input and ceased to allow intermittent, ongoing participation, he undermined his own laudable efforts and unintentionally opened the door for intervention by people who wanted to circumvent his innovative approaches to systemic change.

Inclusiveness is not a one-time or short-term behavior. It is a way of being. There are times, of course, when quick action and prompt decision making are essential. Naturally there must be clear limits to talking, brainstorming, and inclusion. The distinction, however, is whether inclusiveness is an ongoing norm or simply a perfunctory activity to execute and then check off of a to-do list. When inclusiveness is seen as the latter, it has little or no positive impact.

A plethora of other competencies or skills also support the broad visions of this book and, specifically, the contexts that support catalytic conversations, the transformation of differences into resources, emergent thinking, and innovation. For example, talking in a mode of inquiry more than in a mode of advocacy involves asking open questions, telling concise stories, and listening carefully for new understanding. Through these kinds of conversations, people are able to access their cognitive frames of reference in combination with other ways of learning, such as accessing their tacit knowledge. They can tap into emotional connections and discover common experiences that they did not realize before. Embedded in the social, collective environments of intertwined relationships are the recursive movements of tacit, implicit, and explicit knowledge. Through storytelling, participants can transform their tacit knowledge through interaction with the tacit knowledge of others as it enters a collective reservoir out of which they can discover new explicit knowledge. Because people often converse out of their own background and experience, storytelling opens new lines of communication and understanding and can help bridge barriers of differences.

Developing the capacity for constructive controversy is a vital approach, although it is not intended to be the solution for all problems. It is just one way to engage in catalytic conversation. It is an example of an approach that requires participants to surface and constructively deal with their differences as they seek to learn, be surprised, and gain new understanding. Constructive controversy is a way to talk about differences with an open mind and a high degree of respect (see Chapter 5). The primary purpose cannot be to get one's way, to be right, or to dominate. Instead, in constructive controversy, people commit to staying in conversation and continue to revisit issues. They ask questions and genuinely listen to the answers as they strive for better understanding.

People remain engaged with each other over time to work through conflicts, rather than rushing into compromise or coercion. The new information, knowledge, and understanding that are uncovered contribute to the emergence of new alternatives and more creative ways of thinking. Thus, the differences can develop into positive resources for the participants' learning and well-being and for the organizations' improved quality and innovation.

A caution: These interactions are often intense because it is inevitable that strong differences in point of view, positional power, values, and priorities, for example, emerge. While most people can learn to participate effectively in this kind of interaction, many must first develop and practice the necessary competencies. Typically academic settings or professional development and training programs within organizations do not teach many of the competencies most needed or ensure that people adequately practice them.

Because the conversational processes set forth in this book are not a technique or model to implement through predictable steps, they require conceptual knowledge and experiential components for learners to increase their awareness and to practice. Because the learning needed does not all lend itself to didactic work, initially it may seem time consuming. Yet, with minimal experience people begin to see how much more time they waste without the front-end work of developing competencies for substantial catalytic conversation. For example, have you ever left a meeting or project planning session knowing that it did not go well and that participants did not talk adequately about important issues? Have you ever left one of these meetings wishing that you knew how to change these unconstructive patterns? I hope this book helps readers develop conversations of inquiry that catalyze more constructive interactions.

Conclusions

Conversations and relationships flow within a natural rhythm of understanding and misunderstanding (see Chapter 4). When relationships are strong and when intentionality and respect are resolute, misunderstandings serve as catalysts that spark people's interests, ideas, and imagination.

Participants in catalytic conversation bring their individual and collective origins and priorities into their conversations and are able to grapple with differing perspectives and incorporate new aspects of them. They bring forward their own values, wisdom, and knowledge as they adapt. They then selectively either incorporate what they have discovered or at least learn to understand one another better. In the words of David Mathews (1995), who has been deeply involved in civil discourse, people "may not change their own opinions about an issue, but they are quite likely to change their opinions of other people's opinions" (p. 28). It is through seeing other people and their opinions differently that understanding can grow and people can work together more constructively. As we understand more about how others come to think and feel the way they do, the possibilities for respect and learning expand.

While these approaches do not mean one must agree with others or give up one's beliefs or opinions, they are markers of a shift away from less conscious, less intentional, common norms. With the necessary competences and skills in conducive environments, new kinds of interactions can become relatively dependable. Without agreeing or abandoning cherished values and beliefs, we can communicate in a spirit of respect and openness with a mindset committed to continuous learning. For instance, if I want you to understand me better, I have to mirror that intention through seeking new understanding of you. If I want to influence you, I must be open to being influenced by you. Another way to express this approach is to say that I, as a wooer, must be willing "to be wooed" (Heinrichs 1995, 42). The new administration in the United States in 2009 is providing a living example of the challenges and the potential of striving to have influence while being influenced, of articulating new directions while listening to learn from others.

A knowledge-intensive world is the prime place for this work because the medium through which people work is the medium of ideas and knowledge. The most vital raw materials are ideas, knowledge, communication, and relationships—not natural resources such as coal or land. External pressures, global opportunities, and social networks continuously interact, setting the stage for uncertainty. These factors are always in flux as people change, politics and economies shift, environments evolve, time passes, and new technologies develop. Organizational and societal life is an ever-evolving assortment of socially constructed realities.

Work in these complex environments thrives on the capacity for self-organizing and emergent actions that arise out of local interactions among people working together. A primary assumption of this book is that differences among people can be resources for expanding perspectives, knowledge creation, increased humanity, and meaningful innovation. As we discovered, *intent* is the nexus between bringing differences into organizational conversations and benefiting from them. Likewise, respect must be an ever-present part of the air that we share together.

References

Baker, A., P. Jensen, and D. Kolb. 2002. *Conversational learning: An experiential approach to knowledge creation.* Westport, CT: Quorum Books.

Bijlsma-Frankema, K., B. Rosendaal, and Y. Taminiau. 2006. Acting on frictions: Learning blocks and flows in knowledge intensive organizations. *Journal of European Industrial Training* 30 (4): 291–309.

Edmondson, A. 2003. Managing the risk of learning: Psychological safety in work teams. In *International handbook of organizational teamwork and cooperative working,* ed. M. A. West, D. Tjosvold, and K. G. Smith, 255–275. West Sussex, England: John Wiley & Sons, Ltd.

Heinrichs, J. 1995. How Harvard destroyed rhetoric. *Harvard Magazine* (July–August): 37–42.

Jacobs, C. D., and L. T. Heracleous. 2005. Answers for questions to come: Reflective dialogue as an enabler of strategic innovation. *Journal of Organizational Change Management* 18 (4): 338–352.

Mathews, D. 1995. Building a strong civil society and a healthy public life. *Connections.* Dayton, OH: Kettering Foundation.

Morgan, G. 2006. *Images of organization.* Thousand Oaks, CA: Sage Publications.

Nonaka, I. 1994. A dynamic theory of organizational knowledge creation. *Organization Science* 5 (1): 14–37.

Rycroft, R. W., and D. E. Kash. 1999. *The complexity challenge: Technological innovation for the 21st century.* New York: Pinter.

Schon, D. A, 1983. *The reflective practitioner: How professionals think in action.* New York: Basic Books.

Waldrop, M. 1992. *Complexity: The emerging science at the edge of order and chaos.* New York: Simon and Schuster.

Index

About the Author

Ann Baker is an Associate Professor in the School of Public Policy at George Mason University in Arlington, VA. Growing up in the Southeast during segregation influenced her life and work, leading to both academic research and hands-on activism involving finding ways to bridge barriers among people. Building upon her doctoral study at Case Western Reserve University in organizational behavior, she and her two coauthors wrote *Conventional Learning: An Experiential Approach to Knowledge Creation.* In *Catalytic Conversations,* she moves her previous work forward in substantial new ways.